P9-CBU-715

Outlines
in
Irish
History:

Eight Hundred Years
of Struggle

by
Seamus P. Metress, Ph.D.

Copyright © 1995 by Seamus P. Metress
All rights reserved. Printed in the USA
1st Edition: April, 1995

Published by:
Connolly Books
P.O. Box 24744
Detroit, Michigan 48224

Editing and book production: Maria Catalfio

Library of Congress Catalog Card Number: 95-67850

*Special thanks to the
American Committee for Ulster Justice
for funding this project*

TABLE OF CONTENTS

Dedicated to the Irish people
who have struggled for 800 years
for peace, justice and freedom.

Introduction

The history of Irish nationalism is a story full of pathos and passion. But for many years the American public has only heard the official British view of what has happened, and what continues to happen there to this day. This outline attempts to simplify and organize the basic events and trends in the development of Irish nationalism for those who choose to question the established views. It is not meant to be a detailed course in Irish history. However, it is meant for the beginner, and my approach has emphasized the development of a working knowledge of Irish history, rather than adherence to a rigid scholarly form. This text attempts to frame historical sequences, participating groups, individuals and other aspects of the struggle into a picture that makes sense of the complexity that often defines Irish history and politics.

It is hoped that the question and answer format will facilitate self-study. References for further study are included at the end of each chapter in Part I, and Part II ends with an annotated bibliography to encourage further study. The bibliography has a strong Irish republican bias, but also includes sources articulating other viewpoints.

CHAPTER ONE

Origins of the people:
A brief introduction
7500 B.C. – 1014

Pre-Celtic Ireland

1. *What were the earliest inhabitants of Ireland like, where did they come from and where did they first settle in Ireland?*
A. The first settlers arrived in Ireland some time before 7500 B.C.
B. They lived by hunting, fishing, and gathering (pigs, fish, birds, and hazelnuts were important).
C. They may have come from:
   1. Scandanavia by way of Scotland.
   2. France or Spain by way of the south of Ireland.
D. The earliest archaeological sites are mostly concentrated in the northeast of Ireland.
E. Recently, however, sites at Mt. Sandel (Derry), Lough Boora (Offaly), and Carrowmore (Sligo) have challenged the view of a strictly northeastern beachhead.

2. *When did farming arrive in Ireland and from where did it come?*
   The first farmers probably arrived around 3500 B.C. from northern France. The megalithic tombs such as New Grange, Knowth and Dowth were built during this period. One of the most important archaeological sites from this period was Lough Gur in county Limerick.

3. *When did the Bronze Age come to Ireland and what group possibly introduced it?*
A. The Bronze Age was introduced about 2100 B.C. and spread rapidly.
B. By 1500 B.C. an overseas trade in ornaments

and weapons had become important.
1. Ties were established with such places as Egypt and the Baltic.
2. Irish copper and gold from the Wicklow hills were used as raw materials throughout Europe.
C. These innovations may have been introduced to Ireland by an archaeological group known as the Bell Beaker people.
1. The earliest Beaker sites are Ballynagilly, Tyrone (2100 B.C.) and New Grange, Meath (2100 B.C.).
2. They became established between 2100 B.C. and 1300 B.C.
3. The Bell Beaker people were related to the Kurgan culture of Europe (which some scholars associate with Celtic).
D. The Bell Beaker people may have been:
1. The carriers of the Kurgan culture
2. The first Indo-European speakers
3. Possibly the first Celts.
E. This was the last massive invasion of Ireland.

4. *What was the last pre-Celtic group to invade Ireland?*
A. Around 1200 B.C. a group with short heavy swords arrived and built small fortified dwellings in the bogs called crannogs.
B. Possibly they were Picts (but they may have even been Celts).

Celtic Domination

1. *Describe the nature of the Celtic expansion into Ireland.*
A. Between 450 B.C. and 200 B.C. the Celts were the most powerful people in Europe.
B. They expanded into Ireland sometime between 600-200 B.C., probably 500 B.C.
C. It would appear that two movements took place:
1. From north through Scotland and Britain to northeast Ireland.

     a. From the low countries and north-
         west France.
     b. Hallstadt axe Iron Age culture.
  2. From the continent directly to the west
     of Ireland.
     a. From Switzerland and southern
         France (500-400B.C.).
     b. La Tene influence with curvilinear
         design and chariots (150-100B.C.).
D. The Celts pushed the earlier people both north
    and south as they advanced with both clashes
    and mixing taking place.
E. The Celts (Gaels) called Ireland *Erin* after the
    name of the first people they conquered, the
    Eirann (some think they were Picts).

2. ***What is meant by the concept "Cumulative Celticity"?***

It explains the Celtic conquest of Ireland as a series of "invasions" each being a patchwork of conquest, introducing new masters and colonists to settle here or there throughout the country but at the same time leaving the previous populations in place.

3. ***What were some major sociopolitical charac-teristics of the Celts?***

A. They were a pastoral people living on isolated
    farmsteads called raths.
B. They were characterized by rigid social classes
    such as:
  1. Chieftains (nobles).
  2. Freemen (27 classes).
  3. Slaves.
  4. Brehons (law), Druids (religion), Bards
     and Fili (poets).
C. The power of the kingship was based on
    wealth, especially cattle, but the kingship was
    elected.
  1. Tuath was the kingdom and Ireland
     had 97 separate tuaths.
  2. Wars were fought over cattle.
  3. Little centralized authority or power.
D. Authority and ownership were separate con-

cepts, thus being king did not mean ownership of the land.

4. *What were some of the major sociocultural
characteristics of the Celts?*
A. They were sensitive to the rhythms of nature
and exhibited great respect for it.
B. Transitions or turning points between times
were sacred, e.g. twilight, samhain (Hallow-
een).
C. Loyalty to family or group was very important.
D. Oral ability was important, e.g. brehons (law
makers), druids (religious people), bards
(storytellers), etc.
E. Women had more rights and power than in
any other western culture, e.g. separation laws,
divorce, etc.
F. Comic tradition was important. Fatalistic and
grotesque mockery, exaggeration, and ridicule were prominent features. The ridicule
was savage.
G. A world view characterized by author An-
drew Greely as "modified dualism"—that is,
living in the profane but always ready for the
sacred to appear, e.g. laughed at death.
H. Complexity was also a Celtic trait.
   1. Complex precise legal tracts.
   2. Elaborate descriptive saga literature.
   3. Complicated rhyming of the early
      poetry.
   4. Art designs characterized by designs
      within designs.
      a. Spirals, curves, geoforms.
      b. Human or animal representa-
         tions were drawn in highly stylized,
         non-realist forms.
I. Lack of centralization and political cohesion.
   1. Celts did not consider these character-
      istics as necessarily good.
   2. Coordination rather than consolidation
      was the key.
   3. Celtic lack of unity made them
      difficult to conquer since one or two
      victories over them could not be

4

decisive. There was not one Ireland to conquer but many.
4. But Ireland was actually more cohesive than England at this time period.
J. Land belonged to the extended family (or Fine).
1. No individual ownership.
2. Led to fierce resistance because the group, not the individual, lost.

5. Why were the Irish Celts called Gaels?

A. Gaelic is one of the two major divisions of the Celtic language, the other division was called Brythonic.
B. Gaelic includes: Irish, Scots and Manx. Brythonic includes: Welsh, Cornish and Breton.
C. Gaelic speakers cannot understand Brythonic speakers.

6. What did the Gaels (Celts) give to Ireland?

A. Common language.
B. Common religion (druidism).
C. Common culture.
1. Sagas.
2. Brehon laws (p. 14).
3. Bardic poetry and music.
4. Social structure.
5. Food (milk, oats, barley bread, game).
D. The idea of Ireland as a single entity:
1. Irish mythology is dominated by the theme of the security and integrity of the land of Ireland, not one or the other of its constituent parts.
2. Division into five parts or *Cuigeadh*— in old Irish literally means one-fifth, thus a fraction presupposes a whole; the five provinces are conceived as fractions of a single all-embracing totality coterminus with the land of Ireland.
3. The pattern was one of a central province with four other peripheral provinces —Meath was central and within it stood the Hill of Uisnech, the mythological center of Ireland.

4. The cult of the center was important in Celtic mythology and the Irish recreated it geographically with the five ancient provinces.

E. Did not contribute centralized political unity — the kings were really tribal chiefs similar to those in Rwanda, East Africa.

Christian Ireland

1. **When and how did Christianity come to Ireland?**
A. Missionaries arrived 600 years after the "main" body of Celts.
B. St. Patrick was not the first (Palladius, and possibly others preceded Patrick) but he had the most impact, arriving in 432 A.D.
C. A plague in 540 A.D. may have aided the completion of Christianization by weakening local beliefs in the old system.
D. Christianity introduced the Latin alphabet and gave Irish a written form in the 7th century.

2. **What characterized the Irish Celtic brand of Catholicism?**
A. Pagan and Christian ideas were fused (syncretism), e.g. sacred sites, sacred days had aspects of both pagan and Christian traditions (Kildare, Croagh Patrick, Samhain).
B. Diocese model did not work.
    1. Population was not concentrated as in Europe.
    2. Each tuath appointed a bishop, often a relative. One hundred or more bishops existed.
C. Private confession replaced public absolution.
D. Dominance of monasticism.
    1. Abbotts became more powerful than bishops by 700 A.D. Bishops had mainly liturgical roles, such as preaching, ordaining and administering the sacra-

ments.
2. Over 70 monasteries were established in the 5th and 6th centuries which became centers of art and learning.
3. Harsh discipline was maintained.
4. Monks fit in with concepts of Celtic familism, i.e. subordinating personal interests to broader family values.
E. Hermits were highly respected.
F. Missionary activity was great and had a large impact on western Europe, e.g. St. Columba, St. Gall began in Ireland and moved to Scotland and the continent.

3. *How did the Edict of Whitby in 664 attempt to curtail the growth of the Irish church?*
A. The pope ordered the Irish to stop appointing their own bishops.
B. Pope ordered them to halt their missionary activity.
C. It started a major decline. In reference to Ireland, English historian Arnold Toynbee said, "It was one of the aborted civilizations of the world."
D. The Roman Catholics won over the Celtic Catholics.

4. *When did the Vikings first start raiding Ireland and why did Ireland prove difficult to conquer?*
A. 795 A.D., first it was the Norwegians later the Danes.
B. Helped destroy much of the rich monastic culture of the 8th century that had made Ireland "The isle of saints and scholars," but were aided by some Irish chieftains.
C. Ireland was difficult to conquer because of:
    1. The absence of population concentrations.
    2. Hundreds of small kingdoms (tuaths).
    3. Rugged geography e.g. mountains, bogs, forests, drumlin belt, etc.
D. The Vikings settled in towns on the coast, e.g. Dublin, Wexford, Cork, Waterford, Limerick.

1. These were under only nominal control of the Irish chieftains.
2. Their links were with the Vikings in Britain, not with Ireland.

5. *How was the power of the Vikings broken?*

A. Brian Boru, a petty chieftain who could not have risen to power in earliest days, emerged as Ard Ri (high king).

B. Between 500-1000 A.D. there was increasing pressure for land leading to:
   1. War.
   2. Increased tenancy.
   3. The decline of cattle as a unit of wealth.
   4. These changes weakened the old Celtic system of power under a few chieftans.

C. This led to some consolidation of power under a few powerful chieftains.

D. Brian was one of those who benefited from these changes and he defeated the Vikings (whom the Irish called Ostmen) and their allies at Clontarf in 1014.

6. *What were the major contributions of the Vikings to Ireland's sociohistorical development?*

A. Introduced an urban tradition to Ireland.

B. Introduced commercial life and international ties with the European mainstream.

C. Inspired the first sense of national political identity as a result of resistance.

D. They intermarried with the Irish and became part of the local population introducing Scandanavian family names such as Anderson, Atkinson etc.

For Further Reading and Study

Aalen, F.H.A. 1978. *Man and the Landscape in Ireland*. Chapters 1, 2, 3, and 4. Academic Press, New York.

Cunliffe, B. 1979. *The Celtic World*. McGraw-Hill, New York.

dePaor, M. and L. dePaor. 1964. *Early Christian Ireland*. Thames and Hudson, London.

Evans, E. 1966. *Prehistoric and Early Christian Ireland: A Guide*. Barnes and Noble, NY.

Harbison, P. 1988. *Pre-Christian Ireland: From Settler to the Early Celts*. Thames and Hudson, London.

Harbison, P. 1976. *The Archaeology of Ireland*. The Bodley Head, London.

Herity, M. and G. Eogan. 1977. *Ireland in Prehistory*. Allen University, London.

MacNiocaill, G. 1972. *Ireland Before the Vikings*. Gill and Macmillan, Dublin.

O'Kelly, M.J. 1989. *Early Ireland: An Introduction to Irish Prehistory*. Cambirdge University, Cambridge.

CHAPTER TWO

The Norman invasion
1170-1318

1. Who were the Normans?

A group of people led by William the Conqueror who invaded England from France. They defeated the Saxons at Hastings in 1066 and took control of England. They originally came from the province of Normandy in France, but were of mixed Viking and French ancestry. The Normans who invaded Ireland in 1169 were largely a group of landless barons of Welsh-Norman extraction. However, they were French speaking, not English.

2. How did the pope establish the basis for the Normans claims to the lordship of Ireland?

In 1156 Pope Adrian IV (an Englishman) issued the Bull of Laudabiliter which granted the lordship of Ireland to Henry II, King of England. Pope Alexander III confirmed Henry II's right to conquer Ireland.

3. What was the Donation of Constantine?

A document in which the 4th century Roman Emperor Constantine bequeathed jurisdiction over the whole earth to the pope. It was later proven to be a forgery, but it became the legal basis for the pope granting the overlordship of Ireland to Henry II of England.

4. Why was the pope supportive of a Norman invasion of Ireland?

A. To teach traditional "Roman Catholicism" to the "pagan" Irish Catholics.

B. To ensure that the Peters Pence, a special collection for the pope, would be sent to Rome with greater regularity.

C. One king, one church seemed to be a papal

objective.

D. This is the beginning of a long tradition of the pope asking the Irish to obey an English king.

5. *For what reasons did the Normans first invade Ireland?*

A. Diarmid McMurrough, an Irish chieftain, had been deposed after a wife-stealing dispute with the O'Rourkes of Brefni.

B. He fled from Ireland to England and swore fealty to Henry II.

C. He asked Henry for help in regaining his lands.

D. Henry wanted to get rid of some of his more troublesome barons so he granted Diarmid's request by sending Richard De Clare, the Earl of Pembroke, Wales (he was most commonly called Strongbow) to Ireland.

E. Strongbow invaded Ireland in 1170.
   1. He took Wexford and Waterford in August of 1170.
   2. He then married McMurrough's daughter Eva.
   3. He captured Dublin from the Vikings (Ostman) in September of 1170 and then proceeded to sack the city.

6. *Why were the Normans militarily successful?*

A. The Irish chieftains were divided.

B. The Norman forces were professional soldiers, with superior weaponry, e.g. heavy battle axes, long bows, etc.

C. Normans fought in armor on horseback with saddles and stirrups, while the Irish fought on foot without armor.

7. *How did Strongbow and Henry come into conflict over Ireland?*

A. Strongbow claimed all Leinster and the title of Ard-Ri (high king).

B. Henry II crossed over to force the homage of his barons and the Gaelic chiefs.

C. The papal legate forced the Irish chiefs to submit to Henry.

D. However due to different ideas of authority and ownership, the Irish recognized his authority but not his ownership of the land, as was the rule under the feudalism commonly practiced in England. In Ireland the land belonged only to the extended family, not the individual.

8. *Characterize the nature and progress of the Norman settlement of Ireland.*

A. The walled cities were retained for the crown (each with a castle).

B. They re-populated Dublin and the county around it with people from Bristol, England and established small country estates for the lords.

C. Only those Irish willing to become English in dress, language, and customs were allowed in the crown areas or "The Pale." By 1172 the Normans controlled most high church offices.

D. By 1250 the Normans had overrun most parts of Ireland, with the exception of Ulster.

E. But the Irish could not be brought to heel with one military defeat because they lacked centralized political administration.

9. *What was the "Pale"?*

A 20 mile area around Dublin that was surrounded by a double ditch six feet deep and a palisade. It was the main area controlled by English loyalists. It was under constant threat and attack by the Irish chiefs and "Anglo-Irish" who controlled the land outside the "Pale" — counties Dublin, Meath, Louth and Kildare.

10. *How did Gaelic assimilation of the Normans take place and what were its major effects?*

A. Emigration from England stopped.

B. Due to a shortage of labor, the Normans allowed the Irish to return to work their former lands.

C. The Norman lords began to marry the Irish.

D. Within a generation the succession was dominated by the half Irish-Norman children.

E. Eventually except for their titles, the Anglo-Irish lords had become clan chiefs and often times acted more Irish than the Irish.

F. They adopted the Irish language and culture.

11. *In what ways did the native Irish attempt to reassert themselves against the Normans?*

A. For about a century and a half the Normans exploited Irish disunity.

B. Eventually the Irish began to retaliate in a variety of ways.
   1. They started to use Norman military strategy and weapons.
   2. They intermarried with and Gaelicized the Normans.
   3. They attempted to form alliances with the Scots especially Robert and Edward Bruce (1315-1318).
   4. They fought a guerilla war and started to reduce the amount of land controlled by the Normans.

C. From the early 14th century to the early 16th century the unassimilated English Normans were confined to the Pale (area around Dublin).

12. *How did England attempt to break the Gaelicization process?*

A. A Parliament at Kilkenny under Edward III son of the Duke of Clarence, passed the Statute of Kilkenny (1366).

B. The statute included:
   1. Intermarriage with the Irish was treason.
   2. Tolerating or submitting to Brehon law was high treason.
   3. Harboring and encouraging Irish minstrels or storytellers would bring heavy fines.
   4. Permitting Irish tenants to hold land by Gaelic tenure or to graze cattle on crown estates could result in forfeiture of the title.

5. The admission of Irish priests to monasteries, benefices, etc. could bring heavy fines.
6. Use of Irish dress, speech, Irish names or cultural expression could result in forfeiture of lands.
7. The practice of coyne and livery was declared an abuse (the right of armies to live off the lands over which they fought).

13. Why did the Statute of Kilkenny fail?

A. It was impossible to enforce.
   1. The 100 years war with France had diverted England's attention.
   2. The Anglo-Normans were divided by local feuds.
   3. The townspeople and feudal lords did not like or trust each other.
B. When Richard II came to Ireland to assert his power he was badly defeated by the Wicklow chiefs.
C. During the 14th and 15th century Gaelicization became complete with most of the older English invaders using the Irish language for everyday speech.

14. What was the most lasting result of the Statute of Kilkenny?

As the first example of apartheid, it helped establish institutionalized racism as a key factor in the attitudes of the English toward the Irish. It was cultural racism but its spirit had a biological component forbidding physical mixture of the two groups.

15. Even though Gaelic Ireland lacked the institutionalized framework to build a nation, in what ways did it exhibit cultural unity?

A. It had a common language and culture.
B. The Brehon laws reflected the values and customs of the whole island. They emphasized collective responsibility and concern for the people and land.
C. The Irish brand of Christianity was unique.

D. Irish art was unique.
E. The Normans were absorbed into the culture and often became more Irish than the Irish.
F. Ireland at this time was more culturally cohesive than England.

16. What are some of the major Irish family names that were originally Norman?

Burke, Cusack, Dillon, Nagle, Power, Roche, Fitzgerald, Fitzhugh, Prendergast, Butler, Lacy, Darcy.

For Further Reading and Study

Collins, K. 1991. *The Cultural Conquest of Ireland*. Mercier, Cork.

Dolley, Michael. 1972. *Anglo-Norman Ireland*. Gill and Macmillan, Ltd. Dublin.

Fitzgerald, Brian. 1951. *The Geraldines*. Devin-Adair Co. New York.

Lydon, J.F. 1972. *Lordship of Ireland in the Middle Ages*. University of Toronto Press, Toronto.

Moody, T.W. and F.X. Martin, ed. 1984. *The Course of Irish History*. Mercer Press, Cork. Chapter 8, 9, and 10.

CHAPTER THREE

The Tudor conquest of Ireland (1485-1603)

1. How was feudalism changing just prior to the Tudor conquest of Ireland?

A. Feudalism with its multitude of independent lords was changing to an absolute monarchy.

B. Feudalism was further weakened by the Black Death in the mid-1300's because of the significant population losses caused by the plague and disruption of social organization.

C. In Ireland the invasion of the Scottish Edward Bruce (1316-1318) helped to weaken feudalism.

D. Wealthy burghers loyal to the English king hired mercenaries to fight the feudal lords, called barons.

E. The crown owned the only artillery which enabled it to attack castles and other strongholds.

F. Thus the separate military powers of the lords were destroyed.

2. What was the attitude of Henry VII and Henry VIII toward Ireland?

A. They tolerated the Anglo-Irish lords, and some like the Fitzgeralds of Kildare had great power.

B. But they wanted to change the defensive status of "the Pale" (page 12, #9).

3. What was Poynings Law?

It was passed in 1494 and decreed that parliament could meet in Ireland only with Royal permission and that the English King and council had to approve any measures proposed. Its passage was further proof that the Statute of Kilkenny and forced anglicization had failed.

4. *How did Henry VIII come to assume the title "King of Ireland"?*
A. In 1540 he persuaded the clan chiefs outside "the Pale" to become vassals and repudiate the pope's authority, e.g. O'Neill (Earl of Tyrone), O'Donnell (Tyrconnell), O'Brien (Thomond).
B. Henry was then named King of Ireland in 1541 by an Irish Parliament dominated by Anglo-Irish barons.
C. But such submissions were not binding on the clan or any new chief since Irish chiefs were elected.
D. These agreements were between individuals, i.e. Henry and the chief, not his clansmen.

5. *What was the impact of Henry VIII's introduction of the Reformation into Ireland?*
A. Church wealth and property was confiscated.
B. The Irish were not papists thus Henry's quarrels with Rome didn't bother them.
C. Theology and liturgy in Ireland did not substantively change, only the temporal power of the church.
D. But it did mark the beginning of a distinct cultural-religious barrier between the two communities, e.g. English (Protestant), Irish (Catholic)
E. Henry wanted to change the defensive status of the "Pale" and established a standing army in Ireland.

6. *How did Henry VIII's successors change their attitudes toward Ireland and how did the Irish react?*
A. England moved toward a more militant Protestantism.
B. The Tudors insisted that the Irish renounce Catholicism to prove their loyalty.
C. The Irish were offended by the threats from England for a number of reasons:
   1. It was an attack on their Irishness (cultural imperialism).
   2. Catholicism had become a symbol of

Irish culture rather than religious belief.

D. Tudor policies led to the Romanization of the Irish Church.

E. The individualistic and patriachial values of the Protestant reformation ran counter to Celtic ideals which stressed communalism and influential positions for women.

7. *What major considerations began to dominate English policy toward Ireland?*

A. The English began to fear Catholic French and Spanish influence in Ireland.

B. Irish policy became dominated by needs for national security.

C. Plantations of English settlers were attempted.
   1. Mary planted Leix and Offaly, and also South Wicklow and North Munster.
   2. Elizabeth planted Munster (Walter Raleigh and Edward Spencer) (1584-1592).
   3. All failed due to lack of settlers and fierce Irish resistance.

8. *Identify the following local rebellions:*

A. **The Rebellion of Silken Thomas** — the Fitzgeralds of Kildare, led by Thomas Fitzgerald, more commonly known as Silken Thomas, son of Garret Og, rebelled in 1534-35 against Henry VIII.
   1. He reacted to the reported death of his father in the "Tower of London" by attacking Dublin.
   2. English artillery was used to batter down the Fitzgerald stronghold at Maynooth. The castle was sacked and put to the sword by English forces.
   3. Silken Thomas was imprisoned and executed with his five uncles in February 1537 (at Tyburn)
   4. He never became a national hero as other martyrs who had opposed the crown.

B. **The Desmond Rebellions**— the Desmonds of Munster rebelled twice for non-nationalistic reasons.
   1. First Desmond Rebellion, 1568-72:
      a. Fitzgerald branch of the Desmonds

        led by James Maurice Fitzgerald.
   b. They were protesting:
      1) The spread of Protestantism.
      2) The claims of an English adven-
         turer, Sir Peter Carew, to their
         lands.
   c. A precedent was established by ap-
      pealing for help to the pope and the
      King of Spain.
   d. Little help was given.
   e. The Desmonds made peace and
      Elizabeth pardoned them.
2. Second Desmond Rebellion, 1579-83:
   a. Received some help from papacy
      and Spain.
   b. Sir Walter Raleigh and Sir Humphrey
      Gilbert played major roles in sup-
      pressing the rebellion leading to the
      devastation of Munster.
   c. In 1583, the Earl of Desmond's head
      was sent to Elizabeth.
   d. Elizabeth used this rebellion as an
      excuse to plant settlers in Munster
      from 1584 to 1592.
   e. 500,000 acres were confiscated and
      given to Englishmen.

9. *Identify the following Irish chieftains:*
A. **Shane O'Neill**— (1560's) Ulster chieftain.
   1. In 1562 revolted against Elizabeth in
      the name of the old Gaelic order.
   2. Controlled most of Ulster.
   3. Began to plot with Mary of Scotland
      against Elizabeth.
   4. He was murdered by the MacDonnells
      of Antrim in 1567.
B. **Hugh O'Donnell**— (1571-1602) Ulster chieftain.
   1. Escaped from an English prison in 1594
      to lead a rebellion in 1595.
   2. After the Battle of Kinsale (1601) he
      travelled to Spain to seek help but was
      poisoned in 1602 by an agent of the
      crown.
C. **Hugh O'Neill**— (1540-1616) Ulster Chieftain
   1. He was Hugh O'Donnell's father-in-law.

2. Like O'Donnell, he hated England.
3. Defeated the English in a number of battles between 1595-1598.
4. Swore allegiance to English rule along with Rory O'Donnell, but later left Ireland, (see The Flight of the Earls, p. 21, #11) beginning a serious decline in the Gaelic order.

10. What was the nature of the Nine Years War (1595-1603) and after initial successes what prevented victory?

A. Led by the O'Neills of Tyrone and the O'Donnells of Tyrconnell the Gaelic chiefs rebelled against the crown.

B. The revolt was actually started by the McGuire family in 1593.

C. The Irish chieftains had modern arms but lacked the cannon necessary to capture the walled cities.

D. Between 1594-98 the Irish won a number of battles culminating in one of Ireland's greatest victories over England, the Battle of Yellowford on the Blackwater River in Armagh.
1. 4000 English dead, and Sir Henry Bagenal killed.
2. The most decisive win over the English ever.

E. In 1599 the Irish killed the governor of Connacht, Sir Clifford Conyers in the Curlew Mountains of Roscommon.

F. Irish guerilla tactics not only defeated the English but demoralized them.

G. Revolts broke out all over Ireland and Elizabeth reacted:
1. Sent the Earl of Essex (1599) who gave up after six months and was beheaded by Elizabeth.
2. Sent Lord Mountjoy (Sir Charles Blount) who pursued a scorched earth policy destroying people, cattle and crops.

H. The Spanish force landed in the wrong place far to the south, so the Ulster chiefs had to march the length of Ireland to join them at

Kinsale.

I. The Irish clans were forced to fight a formal battle much different than their own guerilla style tactics.

J. The Irish began to organize formal regiments like the European states and fight traditional military battles, which was a mistake for such effective guerilla fighters.

11. Why were the Battle of Kinsale and the Flight of the Earls important events in Irish history?

A. The Battle of Kinsale — (1601) it was the decisive battle of the Nine Years War when the Irish and Spanish lost to the English on Christmas Eve 1601. After this defeat Irish resistance became more and more dispersed.

B. The Flight of the Earls — On September 3, 1607, Hugh O'Neill and Rory O'Donnell with 99 followers left Ireland to live in Rome. It was important because:
  1. It ended much of the "Old Gaelic" order.
     a. Destruction of Brehon Law.
     b. Poets began to disappear.
     c. Gaelic culture declined.
  2. They were accused of treason and their lands confiscated.
  3. It left much of Ulster open to plantation.
  4. It is the sociopolitical basis for the current divisions in northeast Ireland today.

12. How was racism emphasized by the Tudors in their dealings with the Irish?

The Tudors constantly depicted the Irish as a savage and inferior, even inhuman people that needed to be civilized. The English saw themselves as civilizers who needed to use extreme measures to humanize the Irish. The roots of modern anti-Irish racism began to flourish during Tudor times.

For Further Reading and Study

Bradshaw, B. 1974. *The Dissolution of the Religious in Ireland under Henry VIII.* Cambridge University, Cambridge, Mass.

Carrey, N. 1976. *The Elizabethan Conquest of Ireland: A Patten Established 1565-76.* Barnes & Noble, New York.

Edwards, R.D. 1977. *Ireland in the Age of the Tudors.* Barnes and Noble, New York.

Hayes-McCoy, G.A. 1967. *The Tudor Conquest (1534-1603).* In: *The Course of Irish History.* T.W. Moody and F.Y. Martin, eds. Mercier Press, Cork. pp. 174-188.

O'Faolain, S. 1942. *The Great O'Neill.* Mercier, Cork.

Quinn, D.G. 1966. *The Elizabethans and the Irish.* Cornell Univ. Ithaca, New York.

CHAPTER FOUR

Plantation of Ulster and the rising of the Irish clans
1603 – 1660

1. *Briefly describe the plantation of Ulster by James I (1603-1625).*
A. After the "Flight of the Earls" (p. 21, #11) James I decided to clear and plant Ulster in 1608-09. The crown confiscated the lands of the O'Neills and the O'Donnells and gave them to Scottish and English settlers.
   1. About 2,000,000 acres with about 500,000 acres cultivable.
   2. In counties Donegal, Fermanagh, Cavan, Tyrone, Derry and Armagh.
B. Did not plant Antrim, Down or Monaghan.
   1. Already inhabited by many Scots who emigrated in the 15th century to north Down and south Antrim.
   2. The glens of Antrim were Catholic and Gaelic.
   3. Monaghan was ceded earlier to the native McMahons.
C. Native Irish were left with less than 1/40 of the land.
   1. 50,000 acres.
   2. The poorest land.
D. Ulster Tenant Right, established by the English crown in 1608:
   1. Protected Scots and English tenants from eviction and guaranteed a financial interest in any land improvement.
   2. The Irish could be evicted at any time without compensation for improvements.

2. *What difficulties were encountered during the plantation?*
A. The native Irish were hostile and aggressive.

B. By 1630 only 8,000 had settled on confiscated land.

C. Only 13,000 Protestants in the whole of Ulster.

D. Speculators bought the unoccupied land and rented it back to the Irish.

3. *How did the Earl of Strafford plan to use Ireland as a power base for Charles I? (1633-1640)*

A. Strafford was appointed by Charles I (1625-1649) as Lord Deputy for Ireland.

B. Strafford became a despot who punished both Catholics and Presbyterians.

C. Thought he could raise revenue in Ireland to make the king independent of Parliament.

D. Thought he could raise an Irish army to use in England.

E. Thought he would placate the Catholics by making some concessions.

F. But he was eventually arrested in England, tried for treason and executed on May 12, 1641.

4. *How did the Earl of Strafford hinder Irish trade?*

A. Tried to kill the major Irish industry (linen).

B. Sold monopoly rights to a company that would have destroyed the small spinners and weavers had it not gone bankrupt first.

5. *What was the nature of the rising of 1641, and why did it fail?*

A. Clans led by Phelim O'Neil rose in rebellion on October 23, 1641 in order to get their lands back.

B. The failure to take Dublin Castle as planned may have cost dearly since it would have provided artillery, powder and weapons for 30,000.

C. Hugh McMahon leaked the plan by careless talk while drinking and was then betrayed to authorities by Owen Connolly (McMahon was captured and beheaded).

D. Reports of massacres of Protestants by Catholics were greatly exaggerated.

E. Catholic Confederation formed in 1642.
1. Set up a supreme council of 24 and an assembly at Kilkenny.
2. Pledged allegiance to the English crown, not the English Parliament.
3. Did not include Presbyterians.
4. Military unity was sacrificed when four province commanders were appointed.
5. Owen Roe O'Neill was the most capable to lead a unified command.

F. Three armies were in the field: the Royalists (fighting for the crown), the Parliamentarians (fighting for the English Parliament), and the Catholic Confederation.

G. The Confederation had two factions:
1. The older Irish who wanted to overthrow the plantation system and freedom for Ireland. Led by Owen Roe O'Neil.
2. The Anglo Irish Catholic who demanded security for their land and property, but not the overthrow of the plantation system. They were intensely loyal to the King.

6. *Who was Owen Roe O'Neill and what were his military accomplishments?*

A. Owne Roe O'Neill was an exiled Gaelic chieftain, the grandson of Hugh O'Neill, who returned from Spain in 1642.

B. He had military experience as an officer in the service of Spain and proved himself a superior field tactician to the English.

C. He had a concept of an independent Ireland without ties to England, rather than only wishing to regain family lands.

D. He defeated the English again and again:
1. At Benburb, June 6, 1646, he defeated a Scots army under Munro, leaving 3,600 dead while losing only 70 of his own men.
2. He drove the Scots from Derry.
3. He dispersed the Catholic Confedera-

tion.

E. It has been suggested that he tried to make peace with the English General Monck.

7. What was the nature of the Monck/O'Neill negotiations?

A. Monck was a Leveller and O'Neill wanted the same for Ireland.

B. Levellers were a radical element in the mid-seventeenth century English revolution who objected to the disparity of wealth and power in society.

C. Some scholars feel the Monck negotiations had no ideological significance but were used to gain time.

D. Cromwell promised the Levellers Royalist lands in Ireland.

E. Thus both the Irish and English revolutions were aborted.
   1. By the Levellers allowing themselves to be bought and side tracked.
   2. By the death of Owen Roe O'Neill.

F. If the Levellers had won control of the English Army, Anglo-Irish relations might have been quite different.

8. Why was the death of Owen Roe O'Neill significant?

A. When Monck broke off talks O'Neill moved south but died on his way to meet Cromwell (1649).

B. He may have been poisoned by English agents.

C. With the death of O'Neill Ireland lost its only leader capable of contesting Cromwell.

D. O'Neill was possibly the first real resistance fighter with a national rather than a tribal vision of Ireland.

9. What was the nature of Oliver Cromwell's invasion of Ireland?

A. He crossed over in 1649 and brutally destroyed Drogheda and Wexford.
   1. One by one Royalist cities surrendered,

those who did not surrender were put to the sword.

2. His army was fiercely papist-hating and was accompanied by Puritan-preachers known as agitators who preached a war of extermination against all things Irish Catholic.

3. Ireland was not going to be a graveyard for Cromwell's reputation as it had been for other leaders such as Essex who had their reputations or lives destroyed in attempts to conquer Ireland.

B. Cromwell left for Scotland in May of 1650.

C. General Ireton (son-in-law of Cromwell) carried on.

1. Galway yielded May, 1652, to end it.

2. 34,000 left for the continent (mostly soldiers).

10. Why is the memory of Oliver Cromwell such an emotionally charged aspect of Irish folk culture?

A. The population of Ireland was reduced between 1641-1652, from 1,448,000 to 616,000, mostly the result of starvation and disease related to Cromwell's activities.

B. No other European conflict of the time period was characterized by such devasting effects on population.

C. Irish Catholics were cleared to west of the Shannon River.

1. Were told to go "To Hell or Connaught" — meaning to die and go to hell, or move as directed to west of the Shannon by May 1, 1654.

2. About 100,000 were sold into slavery in Jamaica, Barbados, etc.

3. Most land was taken out of Irish Catholic hands.

D. The Protestant minority now controlled three-fourths of the Irish land.

1. A new class was created, the "Protestant ascendancy."

2. But a Protestant community was not

created.

E. Cromwell is remembered, but others such as Sir Walter Raleigh, Sir Humphrey Gilbert were also devastating characters in Irish history.

11. *Why did Cromwell's plan for Ireland fail?*

A. Most Englishmen didn't want to live in Ireland.

B. Speculators went to work:
  1. Accumulated large estates.
  2. Created a new land lord class to rule Ireland.

C. The Irish who were needed to work the land gradually returned to their own lands as virtual "serfs."

D. The Irish had survived in bands living in the forests and mountains.

For Further Reading and Study

Clarke, A. 1966. *The Old English in Ireland, 1625-1642.* Cornell Univ., Ithaca NY.

Clarke, A. 1967. *The Colonizations of Ulster and the Rebellion of 1641 (1603-1660).* In: *The Course of Irish History.* T.W. Moody and F.X. Martin, eds. Mercier, Cork. pp. 189-203.

Costigan, G. 1969. *Ireland in the Seventeenth Century.* In: *A History of Modern History.* G. Costigan. Pegasus, NY.

Ellis, P.B. 1975. *Hell or Connaught: The Cromwellian Colonization of Ireland 1652-1660.* St. Martins NY.

Jackson, T.A. 1947. *The Subjugation of Ireland II.* In: *Ireland Her Own.* T.A. Jackson. Cobbett Press, London. pp. 54-75. (Reprinted by International Publishers, 1970).

MacLysaght, E. 1950. *Irish Life in the Seventeenth Century: After Cromwell.* 2nd Edition. Mercier, Cork.

CHAPTER FIVE

The Restoration and the roots of Irish nationalism
1660 – 1798

1. *What was the Restoration?*

It refers to the reestablishment in 1660 of the monarchy in England under Charles II (1660 – 1685).

2. *Did the Restoration improve the lot of the Irish?*

A. Nothing changed.

B. In fact new restrictions emerged.

   1. Land was once again given to friends and supporters of the king (Royalists).

   2. Irish people driven from their lands hid in the forests and bogs constantly attacking and robbing the English aristocracy. They were known as rapparees, e.g. Brennans of Kilkenny, Redmond O'Hanlon of Armagh.

   3. Economic Restraints:

      a. Navigation Act 1663 — forbid exports to America.

      b. 1663–1667 — export of cattle, sheep, and pigs to England prohibited.

      c. 1669 – export of woolen goods to England prohibited.

      d. Later acts attacked the Irish glass and brewing industries.

      e. These and other measures systematically inhibited Irish economic development and made Ireland dependent on England.

   4. Religious persecution:

      a. 1672 – Catholics could not be elected to the Dublin Parliament.

      b. 1678 – Catholics were executed for treason, e.g. Bishop Oliver Plunkett of Armagh (heart and entrails were burned publicly).

3. *How did the rule of English James II (1685-1688) change the policies toward the Catholic Irish?*

A. Because he was the Catholic brother of Charles, the Catholics thought they had hope. He was of French-Scot extraction.

B. He appointed an Irish Catholic, Richard Talbot, the Earl of Tyrconnell.

C. He suspended the laws against Catholics.

4. *How did he alienate the English people?*

A. His ruthless suppression of a rebellion by his half-brother, the Duke of Monmouth (a James too).

B. His suspected sympathy toward Catholicism.

C. The birth of his son (a Catholic) raised the ire of Parliament because there was now a Catholic male successor to the throne.

5. *How did William of Orange come to the throne of England in 1688?*

A. Parliament wanted him to become King, since he was a Protestant. He was of Spanish-Dutch extraction.

B. He was James' II son-in-law; so in 1688 the Whigs invited him and his wife Mary (James' daughter) to replace James II.

C. William landed November 5, 1688, and James II fled to France after being captured and released by William.

D. William and Mary had to agree to two things:
   1. A Bill of Rights for Parliament— Limiting the power of the king.
   2. An Act of Settlement which stated that no Catholic could succeed to the throne or marry an heir to the throne.
      a. Marriage to a Catholic invalidates ones claim to the throne.
      b. The Act of Settlement is still in effect today.

6. *How was Ireland used in the struggle between a James II and William in 1689?*
A. The struggle was really a continental struggle fought in Ireland. It had nothing to do with religion.
B. Richard Talbot refused to recognize William as king and invited James II to claim his crown in Ireland.
C. James landed in Ireland with some French troops in March, 1689.
    1. He was not really interested in Ireland.
    2. He hoped that Bonnie Dundee in Scotland would raise the clans (but he was killed at Killiecrankie).
D. He summoned the "Patriot" Parliament in Dublin on May 7, 1689.
    1. Declared itself independent of the English Parliament.
    2. Declared itself for religious toleration.
    3. Declared tithes could be paid to a church of choice.
    4. Declared the Irish House of Lords as the last court of appeal.
    5. Threatened confiscation of enemy lands.

7. *What were the problems with James attempt to rally Ireland to his cause?*
A. He would not repeal an old law (1494 Poynings Law, p. 16, #3) which gave the crown control over the Dublin Parliament.
B. Since land issues alienated the Tory landowners, no efforts to give land to the masses of Irish occurred.

8. *How did the struggle between James II and William proceed?*
A. Protestant Williamites retreated to two strongholds, Derry and Enniskillen, e.g. the Derry 105 day siege in 1689.
B. August 12, 1689 — the siege of Derry ended in Protestant victory, giving the Protestant cause a great lift.
C. August, 1689 — General Schomberg arrived and by September Ulster was controlled by

William's forces.

D. Louis XIV of France sent 7,000 troops to aid James.

E. William landed at Carrickfergus.

F. At the Battle of the Boyne, July 1, 1690 — William defeated James who showed poor leadership. (Now celebrated on July 12 since a calendar change.)

G. The Pope backed William, and a mass of thanksgiving was said in Rome to honor William's victory.

H. The Irish fought on alone:
   1. Patrick Sarsfield retreated to the Shannon.
   2. At Aughrim on July 12, 1691 the Irish lost a major battle. Commander St. Ruth was killed and a deserter left a pass open so the English could outflank the Irish.
   3. Siege of Limerick by the Dutch General Gunckel lasted until October 13, 1691.
   4. Treaty of Limerick October 13, 1691 provided that:
      a. Irish soldiers could leave to join the French and other countries known as the "Flight of the Wild Geese"(14,000).
      b. Those who remained could return home with no less toleration than under James II.

I. The Irish should have driven both William and James into the sea and used the opportunity to gain their own freedom.

J. Instead the subject people gave their lives in the causes of their enemies because the right of property was more important than individual freedom at this time.

9. *Why did William break the Treaty of Limerick?*

A. The Dublin Parliament, consisting of mostly Protestant landowners, would not ratify it (1692).

B. Parliament confiscated Catholic lands in violation of the Treaty.

C. William was not a fanatic but his followers were, especially the Protestant ascendancy in Ireland.

10. *What were the Penal Codes that began to be established in 1692 and identify some of their major provisions.*
A. They were a series of largely anti-Catholic and anti-dissenter laws.
B. Penal Laws:
   1. Exiled bishops.
   2. Forbade the entry of Catholic priests into Ireland.
   3. Outlawed religious orders.
   4. Restricted movement of clergy.
   5. Could not vote, sit in parliament or be commissioned in the army.
   6. Could not hold government jobs.
   7. Could not practice law.
   8. Could not possess weapons.
   9. Could not purchase property.
   10. Could not establish schools.
   11. A son could become an Anglican and take his Catholic father's land.

11. *What was the real purpose of the Penal Codes and why did they fail?*
A. Designed to demoralize and dehumanize the majority Catholic population.
B. To concentrate land (95%) and political power in the hands of a Protestant ascendancy.
C. To impede Catholic worship in an effort to destroy it.
D. They failed because:
   1. They did not pursue the religious aspects vigorously enough.
   2. Repression inspired reform and revitalization of the Catholic Church.
      a. Led to closer ties with Rome.
      b. By the end of the 18th century the church was stronger than ever.
   3. Catholicism became identified with being Irish (culturally even more than religiously).

12. How did the Penal Codes aid the cause of Irish nationalism?

A. Completed the division of Ireland into two communities:
   1. Reduced the Catholics to illiterate impoverished serfs.
   2. Protestant ascendancy owned 95% of land, plus held political power.
B. Regenerated the Irish nationality among the poor by:
   1. The poverty experience common to all.
   2. The language persecution of the Irish language and religion.
   3. Arrogance of the Protestant ascendancy in the use of their political power.
C. By the turf fire at night the ideals of old were preserved for the future, by poems, songs and stories.

13. What was the nature of the 18th century agrarian secret societies?

A. They were localized groups of vigilantes who used violent intimidation such as burnings, maiming of cattle and assaults to protest injustice.
B. They were largely protesting high rents and tithes paid to the Protestant church and dues to their church.
C. They mainly dealt with local grievances without a concept of nation (in the north some were even sectarian).
D. They did force some reduction of obligations from the church and landlords.
E. In most areas they harassed both Catholic and Protestant landlords.
F. Examples: Whiteboys, Defenders, Molly Maguires, Capt. Moonlight, Peep-O-Day Boys.

14. How did the largely Anglican Protestant ascendancy come to clash with the Protestant "dissenters" such as the Presbyterians?

A. The ascendancy alienated and degraded their former allies by the 1704 Test Act.

B. 1704 Test Act – not as harsh as Penal Codes, but the civil rights of dissenters were attacked.
   1. Dissenters excluded from public employment (civil or military).
   2. Presbyterian schools closed.
   3. Presbyterian ministers denied right to marry.

C. Economic restrictions on Irish development affected the dissenters greatly since they were often shopkeepers, artisans, skilled craftsmen, etc.

D. It led to much emigration to U.S. e.g. in 1727 3,000 people emigrated from Ireland. By 1769 the number had increased to 44,000.

E. It resulted in a lasting bitterness against England even in America and led to major Irish Presbyterian support for the American Revolution.

F. An epitaph on a Presbyterian tombstone in the Shenandoah Valley of Virginia is revealing "Here lies John Lewis who slew the Irish lord and left Ireland and then raised 7 sons to fight the American Revolution."

For Further Reading and Study

Ellis, P.B. 1975. *Hell or Connaught: The Cromwellian Colonization of Ireland, 1652-1660.* St. Martin's NY.

Ellis, P.B. 1976. *The Boyne Water.* St. Martins, NY.

Jackson, T.A. 1947. *The Subjugation of Ireland III.* In: *Ireland Her Own.* T.A. Jackson. Cobbett Press, London. pp. 76-92.

Simms, J.G. 1967. *The Restoration and Jacobite War (1660-1691).* In: *The Course of Irish History.* T.W. Moody and F.X. Martin, editors, Mercier, Cork. pp. 189-203.

Wall, M. 1967. *The Age of the Penal Laws.* In: *The Course of Irish History.* T.W. Moody and F.X. Martin, eds. Mercer, Cork. pp. 217-221.

CHAPTER SIX

The Rising of 1798 and union with Britain in 1801

1. *Briefly characterize the socioeconomic conditions in 18th century Ireland.*
A. The amount of land under tillage declined.
    1. This was the result of the passage in 1736 of a statute that exempted pasturage from tithes.
    2. This led to a reduction in the amount of land available for use by Irish peasants.
B. Profits from Irish agriculture were rarely reinvested in Ireland.
C. Poor tenants were subject to the practice of "rack renting" (exorbitant) in order to extract the maximum profits from the land.
D. The poverty of the Irish peasants forced an over dependence on a single crop: the potato.
    1. Famines became common 1729–1740.
    2. 1740–41 was called "the year of the slaughter" – 400,000 starved.
E. Absenteeism – meant the landlord lived far from the scenes of misery and oppression.
    1. Couldn't appeal to basic morality.
    2. Often left to the mercy of unscrupulous "agents."
F. Tithes to the Anglican church – everyone was compelled to pay regardless of religious affiliation.
    1. The Irish thought the Anglican church heretical.
    2. The church was often an absentee landlord too, e.g. Clare — there were 67 parishes without a church that still collected tithes.

2. *Explain the rise in agrarian violence in the 1760's?*
A. Secret societies such as the Whiteboys, Oak

boys and Steelboys were again organized to protect against excessive rents and tithes.

B. They used violent intimidation with few killings, but did much damage to property.

C. The Catholic church condemned it although some parish priests supported it.

D. Both Catholic and Protestant landlords were attacked if unjust.

E. Both Catholic and Protestant laborers participated.

F. In the north it became sectarian:
   1. Battle of Diamond (Armagh), September 21, 1795. Defenders (Catholic) vs. Peep-O-Day Boys (Protestant).
   2. Grand Orange Order of Ulster founded (p. 108, #19 and p. 139, #1).
   3. Drove many Catholics out of Ulster.

G. Some people emigrated to avoid agrarian violence.

3. *Who were the Irish Volunteers and what kinds of concessions did they force from Britain?*

A. While Britain was busy in America and a French threat existed on the continent, the Volunteers were formed in 1778 to protect Ireland from a possible French invasion.

B. The Irish Volunteers were exclusively Protestant.

C. The Volunteers proved they could successfully wield political and military clout and forced concessions from Britain:
   1. Free Irish Parliament Act of 1783:
      a. Repealed Poynings Law (p. 16, #3).
      b. Repealed Declaratory Act of 1719.
   2. Ended British mercantilism in Ireland (1779–1780).

D. Dungannon Convention, February 15, 1782 – affirmed that only Dublin could legislate for Ireland.

4. *Why do some historians characterize Ireland as a nation in the years 1782-1800?*

A. An independent and exclusively Irish Protestant Parliament existed. However:

1. It would not help the Catholic masses.
2. Most members were land owners who opposed land reform.
3. Henry Grattan and Henry Flood, both prominent members of this Parliament, favored complete freedom of worship and admission of propertied Catholics to Parliament.

B. Grattan once said "the Irish Protestants could never be free till Irish Catholics ceased to be slaves."

5. *What were some concessions to Irish Catholics that were probably brought on by the French Revolution?*
A. They were allowed to operate schools.
B. They were allowed to practice law.
C. Catholic Relief Bill of 1793.
    1. Allowed them to vote if their property produced 40 shillings a year in taxes.
    2. Allowed to hold military commissions below colonel.
    3. Allowed to serve on juries and municipal corporations.
D. In 1795 Parliament endowed New Seminary at Maynooth.
    1. 9,000 pounds a year.
    2. Hoped to train a clergy free of the continental radical ideology.
    3. Church hierarchy was grateful and cooperative.
E. But no agrarian reform.
    1. 1782: found three-fourths of the Irish as virtual slaves.
    2. The government was in the hands of a privileged few.

The United Irishmen 1791-1800

1. *What was the nature of those who founded the United Irishmen?*
A. Anglo-Irish people who were dissatisfied with the Irish parliament which was too biased toward the aristocracy.
B. Protestant dissenters who admired France and

the French Revolution.

C. People who admired Patrick Henry, Samuel Adams and other American revolutionaries.

D. Founded in Belfast in 1791 at the instigation of Theobald Wolfe Tone.
   1. The founders McCracken, Tone, Russell, the Sheares, took a vow on Cave Hill in Belfast to free Ireland.
   2. Thomas Paine's attack on Burke's *Reflections on the French Revolution* – *The Rights of Man* – was called the Koran of the United Irishmen.
   3. *The Northern Star* edited by Samuel Nielson was the militant mouthpiece.

2. *What were the goals of the United Irishmen?*
A. An independent Ireland.
B. Democratic franchise for all.
C. Catholic participation in government.
D. Reform of the Irish political system e.g. abolish the "rotten" burroughs which consisted of representational districts wholly owned by a few wealthy families.
E. No agrarian proposals even though they hoped for the support of the "men of no property."

3. *Why is Theobald Wolfe Tone considered the founder of Irish republicanism?*
A. He advocated an independent non-sectarian republic for Ireland.
B. Since boyhood he questioned the British presence in Ireland.
C. He also insisted the separation from England would be achieved by the use of physical force.
D. He became one of Ireland's first nationalist martyrs.
E. The French Revolution greatly affected him.
   1. Its ideals inspired him to promote a non-sectarian democracy.
   2. It gave him a broad rather than provincial perspective and enlarged his sym-

pathies to include the oppressed of other nations (like the IRA today).
3. The American Revolution influenced him.

F. Modern devotion to the ideals of Wolfe Tone and the United Irishmen begins in 1843.
1. Young Irelander Thomas Davis, after a visit to Tone's grave, wrote a poem *The Grave of Wolfe Tone.*
2. The Young Irelanders (p. 54, #15) revived the memories of Tone and his comrades of 1798.
3. Each year on the 3rd Sunday of June there is a pilgrimage to his grave at Bodenstown, Kildare

4. What was the earliest evidence of a Rising and how did the crown react?

A. Early hints at rebellion:
1. A French force appeared in Bantry Bay in 1796.
2. This fired up the peasants and they started to drill and arm.

B. The crown reaction:
1. They assigned 70,000 troops and an equal number of local militia to Ireland (more than they used against Napoleon).
2. They used informers and arrested a number of the leaders of the United Men.
3. They moved largely Catholic troops into Ulster to stir up sectarian passions among Catholics and Protestants.
4. They sent General Gerald Lake to Ireland.
   a. He was cruel and inhumane.
   b. Used burnings, lootings, floggings and executions, e.g. hung William Orr as an example 1797.
   c. Sir Ralph Abercombie resigned as Commander-in-Chief in March 1798 because of the breakdown of military discipline.

5. *How did the British disrupt much of the Rising plan?*
A. British aborted much of the plan set for May 23, 1798.
B. Through the use of informers they arrested many of the leaders.
C. 34 of the original members died eventually on the gallows.
D. Lord Edward Fitzgerald (the major military leader for the United Men forces) was captured and wounded, and died on May 4, 1798.

6. *What were the actual military engagements like?*
A. It started in Leinster where 350 Irish peasants fought, died and were buried in a mass grave on the Hill of Tara, e.g. croppies grave.
B. At Boolavogue, Wexford, on May 26 a spontaneous rising led by the local priests began:
   1. Most successful (using pikes, pitch forks, etc.).
   2. Took Wexford, Enniscorthy, and actually controlled the whole county.
   3. The rebels failed to take advantage of the early successes.
   4. They were finally overwhelmed on June 13, 1798, at Vinegar Hill by General Lake with 13,000 troops after a savage fight.
   5. British response was excessive:
      a. Floggings, torture, hanging.
      b. Pitch capping, crucifixion.
      c. Lord Morley claimed it exceeded the 1792 massacres in Paris.
      d. Lord Cornwallis, Lord Lt., was appalled at the brutality of it.
C. Dublin had been placed under martial law and systematically repressed.
   1. This prevented an outbreak in Dublin.
   2. Such an outbreak might have led to a linking up with Wexford and the out come of the rising might have been different.
D. In Ulster there were risings in Down and Antrim led by Henry Munro and Henry Joy

McCracken but after early successes they fell to superior numbers and fire power.

7. **What was the nature of French involvement in the Rising of 1798?**
A. The aid was poorly timed and uncoordinated.
B. French General Humbert landed at Killala, August 22, 1798.
   1. Initially successful with peasant support e.g. the Races of Castlebar when he chased a retreating British Army 60 miles to Athlone.
   2. But surrendered when outnumbered 20 to 1 at Ballinamuck, Longford. The French were accorded POW treatment, but the Irish were lined up and bayonetted one after the other.
   3. Led to new atrocities against the peasantry.
C. French Admiral Bonpard arrived with nine ships and 3,000 men in November of 1798.
   1. But lost a naval battle on Lough Swilly.
   2. Wolfe Tone was captured:
      a. Tried for treason.
      b. November 19, 1798 – took his own life? Or did the British do it and make it look like suicide?

8. **Why was the 1798 Rising a military failure for the Irish?**
A. The use of informers to arrest the major leaders.
B. The massive presence of British troops.
C. Bad weather that affected operations of the French fleet.
D. Failure of many Catholics and Protestants to cooperate.
E The class interests between the rich and the poor did not coincide over the issue of private property.

9. **What was the significance of the 1798 Rising?**
A. It has been said that no single event since Cromwell has impressed itself so deeply on

the Irish consciousness.
1. Passed on from generation to generation by tales, poems and songs.
2. Fueled a bitter hatred of the British ruling class.
B. The Young Irelanders (p. 54, #15) revived the memory of 1798 after O'Connell tried to snuff it out.
C. In 1913 Padriac Pearse referred to Bodenstown (the site of Tone's grave) as the holiest place in Ireland.
D. The 1798 rising produced the basic ideals that guide the revolutionaries today toward a free, democratic, non-sectarian Ireland.

The Union of Ireland and Britain

1. *Why did William Pitt wish to bring about the union of Ireland and Britain?*
A. He regarded the rising of 1798 as an act of treason.
B. He thought union was in Britain's best interest in order to control the rebellious Irish.

2. *Identify the opponents and supporters of William Pitt's proposed union.*
A. Opposition to Union:
1. Anglo-Irish patriots who feared for Ireland's economic and political interests.
2. Orange Lodges who did not want concessions to Catholics.
B. Support for the Union:
1. Anti-Catholics who felt that the crown was necessary to protect Protestant interests.
2. Those who feared Catholic agitation and French ideology more than the Protestant ascendancy (middle class Protestants).
3. Catholic hierarchy and aristocracy;
a. Who hoped for emancipation.
b. It would not have succeeded with-

43

out the support of the hierarchy.
  c. Henry Grattan (p. 38, #3) on the
      bishops: "a band of prostituted men."
C. To the ordinary Irish peasant it meant nothing.

3. *How did William Pitt succeed in passing the
   Act of Union in 1801?*
A. He knew it would be hard to convince the
   Irish Parliament to do away with itself.
   1. He bought most support.
   2. He hinted at Catholic emancipation.
B. Passing the Act:
   1. It passed 158-115 in the House of Com-
      mons but Grattan claimed that all but
      seven votes were bribed.
   2. It passed the House of Lords, 75-26 in
      Lords, but Cornwallis said that half of
      those that voted for it actually detested
      it.

4. *How was Ireland short-changed in the
   implementation of the Union?*
A. Ireland got 100 seats in the House of Commons and 32 in the House of Lords.
B. This was 15 percent of the seats, but on the
   basis of population it should have been 45
   percent since Ireland had five million out of
   the total United Kingdom population of eleven
   million.
C. Church of England and Ireland were united
   into the Church of England even though only
   10% of the Irish supported it.
D. If an election had been held the Act would
   have been defeated almost everywhere.
E. Petitions signed against the Act of Union to-
   taled 170,000. Those for the union numbered
   3,000.
F. The peasants couldn't care less who was ex-
   ploiting them.
G. The crown refused to concede Catholic Emancipation, i.e. primarily voting rights.
   1. Pitt resigned.
   2. Several times the House of Commons

passed the Act of Union but the crown and Lords defeated it.
3. Anti-Irish prejudice worked against passage.
H. Economic dogma was important.
1. Property rights were unassailable.
2. To make an exception in Ireland would be dangerous because it was feared that the Catholic vote could work against property rights.

5. What were the effects of Union?
A. It created a powerful and emotional issue in British politics.
1. Destroyed political careers.
2. Brought down governments.
B. Intensified rather than diminished the ethnic and cultural differences between the two traditions.
C. Governed the two islands in the interests of the wealthy British industrial elite at the expense of Ireland.
1. By 1823 Ireland's share of the national debt of England was 50,000,000 pounds.
2. It rendered Ireland bankrupt.
3. Profits from Irish land were invested in England:
   a. Manufacturing.
   b. Industrialization.
D. Quotes from Englishmen:
1. Byron "The Union of the shark and the prey."
2. Dr. Samuel Johnson "We should unite with you to rob you." (1779)
E. Irish nationalism rose again from the failure of the Union.

6. What was the nature of Robert Emmet's Rebellion of 1803?
A. Emmet was an Irish Protestant who was expelled from Trinity College for subversive activity.
B. He attempted to get French help for another rising.

C. He enlisted the support of Michael Dwyer, a fugitive from 1798, who was still operating in the Wicklow Mountains.

D. On July 23, 1803 he tried to rally the slum dwellers of Dublin.
   1. It was crushed within two hours.
   2. The British then used it as an excuse to loot, burn, and attack women.
   3. 300 were jailed.

E. Dwyer had never received word of the rising in order to act.

F. Emmet escaped but was captured later while trying to see his sweetheart Sarah Curran.

7. *Why did Emmet's trial and execution have a lasting affect on the Irish people?*

A. The Trial – September 1803:
   1. His behavior changed the public mood after he gave a famous speech from the dock. "When my country takes her place among the nations of the earth, then, and not til then, let my epitaph be written."
   2. His lawyer, Leonard McNally, was later found to be an informer (betrayed the United Men too).

B. Execution – September 20, 1803, Dublin:
   1. He was hanged and decapitated in front of St. Catherines Church, Thomas Street.
   2. The people who laughed and scorned him in July took him to their hearts.

C. It is possible no death ever affected the Irish people as that of Emmet:
   1. Michael Collins recited his speech on the eve of 1916.
   2. Copies of the speech were found on cabin walls and children were named after him. Many places bear his name and countless statues have been erected in his honor.
   3. Even Abraham Lincoln read Emmet's speech during his self-education.
   4. Padraic Pearse considered him a hero in the mold of the Irish mythological hero Cuchulain.
   5. Even James Connolly interpreted his

attempt to recruit the weavers and tanners of the slums as a effort to strike a blow for the working class.

For Further Reading and Study

Cronin, S. 1981. *The United Irishmen and Secular Nationalism*. In: *Irish Nationalism*. S. Cronin. Continuum Press NY. pp. 40-64.

Costigan, G. 1969. *Ireland in the Age Revolution*. In: *A History of Modern Ireland*. G. Costigan. Pegasus Press, NY. pp. 113-143.

Jackson, T.A. 1970. *Ireland Her Own*. Chapters 7, 8, 9, 10, and 11. International Publishers, NY.

MacAonghusa P. and L. Reagain ed. 1972. *The Best of Wolfetone*. Mercier Press, Cork.

McDowell, R.B. 1944. *Irish Public Opinion, 1750-1800*. Faber and Faber, London.

_____. 1984. *The Protestant Nation, 1775-1800*. In: *The Course of Irish History*. T.W. Moody and F.X. Martin, eds. Mercier, Cork. pp. 232-247.

O'Connell, M.R. 1965. *Irish Politics and Social Conflict in the Age of the American Revolution*. Univ. Penna., Philadelphia.

Pakenham, T. 1969. *The Year of Liberty: The Story of the Irish Rebellion of 1798*. Haddon and Stoughton, London.

Smyth, J. 1993. *The Men of No Property*. Gill and Macmillan, Dublin.

CHAPTER SEVEN

O'Connell, Emancipation, Repeal and Irish identity
1815-1847

1. Who was Daniel O'Connell?

He was a 19th century liberal Catholic lawyer and member of Parliament. He is often called the "Liberator" but John Mitchel, the Irish nationalist leader, said he was "next to the British government the greatest enemy the Irish people ever had." His approach stressed political action centered around civil rights for Catholics. He was not a pacifist as some revisionists have claimed, since he was an active participant in the suppression of the rebellion of 1798 as a member of the local Protestant militia, the Yeomanry. He also strongly supported the idea of Irishmen serving in the British military.

2. What was the basic political ideology of O'Connell?

He considered himself a philosophical radical like Bentham, Paine or Godwin. But in actuality he was a contradiction to those ideals.

A. He opposed the House of Lords, but he revered the monarchy. He referred to Queen Victoria as "the darling little queen."

B. He helped found the Chartist movement which campaigned for broader voting and political rights in England, but he frequently denounced it, which helped to prevent the coming together of Irish nationalism and the British working class.

C. He was a landlord who cared little for land reform.

D. He supported British laissez-faire industrialism at the expense of Irish agriculture.

E. He was anti-labor union and opposed child labor laws in the mining industry and minimum wage laws.

F. He was progressive on human rights issues such as the abolition of slavery, anti-capital punishment, anti-flogging and Jewish emancipation.

G In reality he used the threat of rebellion by the masses of Irish peasants to get concessions for the Catholic middle class.

3. *What were O'Connell's ultimate goals?*
A. Catholic Emancipation for the middle and upper classes. This primarily meant the right of propertied Catholics to vote and hold office.
B. Repeal of the Union of Britain and Ireland and restoration the Irish Parliament, but with representation for the Irish people, two parliaments and a one-king monarch.
C. He did not favor land reform.

4. *How did O'Connell contribute to the development of an Irish identity?*
A. He converted Catholic identity into an Irish identity but in so doing he drove the Presbyterian nationalists away. This allowed the British to encourage the Presbyterians to become unionists.
B. He deliberately discouraged the use of the Irish language though he was bilingual.
C. The political conservatism of O'Connell spurred the development of the Young Ireland movement (p. 54, #15). The Young Irelanders failed militarily but left behind a written legacy that greatly influenced later generations of Irish nationalists at home and abroad.
D. Some have said that he had every quality to lead Ireland to freedom except the will to revolt.

5. *What was Grattan's compromise of 1815 and why did O'Connell oppose it?*
Henry Grattan (p. 38, #3) wanted to guarantee civil rights for Catholics in the United Kingdom in

exchange for the non-appointment of unfriendly Catholic bishops in England and Ireland.

O'Connell opposed it for basically two reasons. He felt that control over the hierarchy violated his ideas on separation of church and state. More importantly he did not wish to disrupt the link between Irishness and Catholicity. He felt that this was the only issue that moved the Irish masses and also O'Connell's power base.

6. What was the Catholic Association and its plan of action?

It was an organization founded in 1823 by O'Connell, Thomas Wyse and Richard Lalor Sheil to foster Catholic Emancipation. It was hoped that the priests would promote it as a patriotic yet holy organization. Its basic plan of action was to:

A. Establish a demographic power base for agitation.

B. Establish financial base for the movement.

C. Involve the tenant farmer class by creating an associate membership:
  1. Costing 1 shilling a year, paid in part or whole.
  2. This was considerably less than the regular dues of 1 guinea a year.

7. How did the Catholic Association take the offensive in the elections of 1826, 1828?

A. The election of 1826:
  1. It worked to elect Protestants who had opposed the Penal Codes.
  2. Tenant farmers showed up at the polls with their priests.
  3. The Association challenged the Protestant ascendancy such as the Beresford family in Waterford and won.

B. The election of 1828:
  1. O'Connell himself challenged C.E. Vesy Fitzgerald, the Duke of Wellington's choice in Clare and won.
  2. But Parliament would not seat him because he was a Catholic.
  3. This upset the Irish masses and rebellion was in the air which forced the

issue in Parliament.

8. What was the Catholic Relief Act of 1829 and what were its effects?

It removed all restrictions on upper and middle class Catholics holding public office with the exception of the Lord Lieutenancy of Ireland and the Lord Chancellorships of England and Ireland. Its major effects were:

A. Upper and middle class Catholics gained sociopolitical and professional benefits.
B. The peasants remained poor and landless or were forced to live in urban poverty with no political rights. Almost eight million people were left without voting rights.
C. It had repressive aspects:
   1. Outlawed the Catholic Association.
   2. Abolished the vote for 40 shilling free holders.
   3. Raised property qualifications for voting to 10 pounds, which reduced the number of people eligible to vote from 200,000 to 90,000.
   4. Members of Parliament were forced to swear allegiance to the crown.
   5. O'Connell was forced to rewin his seat.
D. It did not abolish the Penal Codes (p. 33, #10) as some have suggested since many had already been repealed by the Catholic Relief Bill of 1793 (p. 38, #5.C.)

9. What was the importance of the Catholic Association?

A. It may have served as a prototype movement for total emancipation in other countries, even England.
B. Irish peasants learned how to use the democratic process and how to manipulate the British political system.
C. Some have suggested that the shilling for dues was a sacrifice that gave people a sense .of belonging, with hope and dignity.
D. However Irish Protestants became more dependent on England for protection and "no popery" became a popular slogan.

51

E. In England it encouraged more intense anti-Catholic feeling.

10. What was the Education Act of 1831 and what were its effects?

It established State supported non-denominational schools.

A. They taught English language, literature and history.

B. It was an attempt to destroy Irish national identity.

C. The schools were second only to the Famine in destroying Gaelic language.

D. The attempt failed for the most part because:
  1. Many of the school masters taught from a nationalist perspective.
  2. The schools did not remain non-denominational long.
  3. By teaching the Irish to read, they could read Irish nationalist as well as British material.

11. What was the Tithe War and how was it resolved?

In 1831-36 people began to withhold payment of tithes to the Anglican Church. The government countered by suspending habeas corpus and sending troops and police to arrest agitators and protect church property. However the resistance continued to spread nationwide. O'Connell feared such mobilization would lead to a violent revolt.

The situation was resolved by the passage of the Tithe Commutation Act of 1838 which reduced tithes by 25 percent and levied them against the owner, not the occupant. However, in many cases the owners raised the rents to cover their costs.

12. How did O'Connell come to found the Repeal Association in 1840?

After ten years of cooperating with Whigs and supporting most of their progressive legislation, O'Connell realized he had been duped. He founded the Repeal Association to bring an end to the Act of Union (p. 44 #3) in an attempt to bring together

52

people who:

A. Opposed to the Irish Poor Law of 1838 which instituted taxes as a means of funding workhouses, but in actuality reduced more people to indigents because they couldn't afford to pay the tax.

B. Resented British misgovernment.

C. Were active in Father Matthews Temperance Movement.

O'Connell organized large public meetings calling for repeal of the Act of Union. However, he mostly played a game of brinksmanship to get concessions and then would back away from following through on his threats.

13. What was the British attitude toward repeal and how did O'Connell respond?

British Prime Minister Robert Peel in 1843 informed O'Connell that Britain would fight to save the union. He threatened the use of massive force. O'Connell backed off and told his followers to obey the law when the crown banned a massive meeting at Clontarf.

O'Connell was jailed but released shortly by the courts. He was welcomed home as a hero, but he had nothing left to mount a new challenge.

14. What were the results of the repeal agitation?

Prime Minister Peel, in order to ingratiate the church, provided the Catholic church with charitable bequests and set up a permanent endowment for Maynooth Seminary. In 1850 one member of Parliament said "a loyal priesthood in Ireland is worth more than a standing army." Peel also established colleges in Cork, Belfast and Galway to provide opportunities in higher education for the middle class.

Finally he set up the Devon Commission to investigate the condition of the peasants. However, these concessions stirred anti-Catholic attitudes in England and strengthened British opposition to land reform. The Catholic Church responded by banning Catholics from attending or teaching at Queens University.

15. What was the Young Ireland movement?

A political movement founded in 1842 by Thomas Davis, John Dillon, Charles Duffy, John Mitchel, James Fintan Lalor and William O'Brien. It stressed cultural nationalism, encouraging the Irish to be more aware of their history, language and traditions. The movement rejected the racism of the Saxon versus the Celt, emphasizing that all can claim Irish nationality. The totality of the Irish experience counted most. *The Nation* became the voice of the Young Irelanders and a source for the mythology, literature and ideology of Irish nationalism.

16. Why did the Young Irelanders split with O'Connell?

A. They opposed his cooperation with the British.
B. O'Connell criticized their praise of 1798 with its use of physical force.
C. In 1846 O'Connell wanted his members to agree to never revolt.
D. The Young Irelanders walked out of Concilliation Hall in Dublin in 1847 and formed the Irish Confederation.

17. Identify the Irish Confederation.

It was an organization formed by the Young Irelanders in 1847 to promote cultural nationalism and harmony among the different religions.

18. Who was James Fintan Lalor and what was his importance?

He was a handicapped farmer from county Laois who, as part of the Young Ireland movement, urged a "moral insurrection" by farmers throughout the 1840s. He suggested that they refuse to pay rents and taxes until family obligations were met. His attack on landlordism and the right of the Irish people to the ownership of Irish land greatly affected the thinking of John Mitchel, Michael Davitt and James Connolly.

19. How was the Irish Confederation split by tactical and ideological differences?

A. One group led by William O'Brien and Charles Gavin Duffy believed in constitutional reform and formed the Irish Parliamentary Party.

B. Another group led by John Mitchel and James Fintan Lalor believed in revolutionary reform and supported non-payment of rents and taxes.

C. Eventually Mitchel began to advocate open revolt. He left the group and founded *The United Irishman* paper, which taught techniques of guerilla warfare.

20. How did the Paris revolt of 1848 effect the Young Irelanders?

The Young Irelanders abandoned the constitutional approach and tried to get help from the Second French Republic. John Mitchel rejoined and prepared for revolt. But Britain, by the coercion and arrest of the leaders, forced a premature revolt on August 5, 1848. The group's middle class orientation was not conducive to revolt; the peasants were starving in the midst of the Famine; and the most effective leaders were in jail. The revolt failed militarily after a brief skirmish in Tipperary. The Young Irelanders did not really have a military organization with arms and ammunition to carry out a revolution.

21. What was the long term significance of the Young Ireland movement?

A. It provided an ideology for the future in both Irish politics and the literary renaissance.

B. It renewed again the right of the Irish people to use force against England.

C. The editorials, essays, songs and poems were the literature of cultural nationalism.

D. The writings of James Fintan Lalor on landlordism became the basis for the Land League and part of the revolutionary writings of James Connolly.

E. Exiles from the movement spread its gospel

of Irish Republicanism to North America and Australia.

F.   It also gave Ireland the tricolor — its flag and symbol of Irish defiance, resistance, and unity to this day.

For Further Reading and Study

Cronin, S. 1981. *The Romantic Nationalism of Young Ireland.* In: *Irish Nationalism.* S. Cronin. Continuum Press, New York.

Duffy, C.G. 1896. *Young Ireland: A Fragment of Irish History, 1840-45.* 2 Vols. Fisher Univer., London.

Jackson, T.A. 1970. *Ireland Her Own.* Chapters 12, 13, 14, 15, and 16. International Publishers, New York.

McCartney, D. 1980. *The World of Daniel O'Connell.* Mercier, Cork.

O'Faolain, S. 1970. *King of the Beggars.* Allan Figgis, Dublin.

O'Tuathaigh, G. 1972. *Ireland Before the Famine 1798-1848.* Gill and Macmillan, Dublin.

Whyte, J.H. 1984. *The Age of Daniel O'Connell (1800-47).* In: *The Course of Irish History.* T.W. Moody and F.X. Martin, eds. Mercier, Cork. pp. 248-262.

CHAPTER EIGHT

The Great Starvation
1846 – 1848

The Prelude to Starvation

1. **How was Ireland exploited to satisfy the needs of 18th century British capitalism?**
A. Prior to 1750:
   1. Irish capital yielded an inflow of capital to England in the form of raw materials, rents, etc.
   2. Ireland provided markets for British manufactured goods and the crown disallowed local competition by granting monopolies in industry and commerce to English concerns.
B. 1750-1800's:
   1. Raw materials from Ireland became essential to English industry and were exchanged unequally for manufactured products.
   2. Low costs of labor and production in Ireland led to cheap foodstuffs for the British industrial classes.
   3. Ireland ended up with a subsistence agriculture combined with commercial agriculture as wage earners provided their own subsistence from dwarf holdings.

2. **What were the socioeconomic characteristics of 18th century Irish agriculture?**
A. Subsistence tenant farmers raised potatoes, turnips, oats for their own consumption, but also grew wheat, rye, barley for export. Landlords reaped the profits from these exports.
B. Two zones within a single holding led to a dual economy:
   1. Cash crops (e.g. wheat, barley, rye).
   2. Subsistence crops (e.g. potatoes, turnips) usually the worst land.

C. Labor service to the landlord was exchanged for dwarf holdings. Those who worked the land were called cottiers.

D. As subsistence crop areas were improved, they were converted to cash tillage in order to meet increased rents and new subsistence zones created.

E. Absentee land owners were often represented by exploitive middlemen.

3. *What were the effects of the socioeconomic structure on 18th century Ireland?*

A. Poorer and poorer land was exploited for subsistence.

B. Economic development of Ireland was blocked.

C. More and more people lived on less and less poor land.

D. The chances of massive starvation increased.

4. *How did the 19th century shift to capital intensive agriculture affect the Irish peasant?*

A. Landlords cleared estates (especially in the most fertile areas).

B. It created a home market for food among displaced peasants who had become wage earners.

C. It helped to augment the industrial reserve "army" of labor for English industry.

D. Evictions were made easier by legislation passed in 1818, 1820, 1826, 1848.

The Potato and the Irish Peasant

1. *What was the nature of the spread of the potato in Ireland?*

A. In 50 years it spread throughout Ireland (first five decades of the early 17th century) while in England it took 250 years.

B. By 1700 it had replaced grain as a staple.

C. Became more important in Ireland than any other European country.

2. **Why did the potato spread so rapidly?**
A. Good soil conditions: deep, friable, acid.
B. Good climate during growing season:
   1. Heavy rain.
   2. Brisk moist winds.
   3. High humidity.
   4. Ocean modified temperatures (20-81 degree F).
C. The absence of ecological enemies such as aphids.
D. It was a cheap, productive food that:
   1. Needed little labor.
   2. Needed little money for seed.
   3. Produced a large yield from small acreage.
E. Its methods of cultivation were easily fitted to the implements already in use: hoe, spade.
F. The system of land tenure encouraged it, e.g. small subsistence plots.
G. Ideally suited to the turbulent sociopolitical conditions of the 17th century, e.g. wars, rebellions, etc.:
   1. Not easily trampled by cavalry.
   2. No warehouses that could be easily destroyed.
H. Fitted the customary cooking methods:
   1. No new utensils needed.
   2. Didn't need more fuel.
   3. Easy to store.

3. **What were the effects of the success of the potato?**
A. Population grew (earlier age at marriage).
B. Individual holdings got smaller.
C. The Irish peasant became more and more dependent on one crop.

Ireland on the Eve of Famine/Starvation

1. **What was the demographic situation?**
A. Population had been increasing steadily since mid-18th century.
   1. 1700 = 2.5 million

      2.   1750 = 3 million
      3.   1800 = 5.25 million
      4.   1841 = 8,175,124 (some scholars think the population might have actually been one-third higher than this figure).

B. Between 1779-1841 Ireland experienced a 172% increase in population, compared to an 88% increase in England.

C. Ireland was the most densely populated country in Europe.

D. The mass of the population was heavily dependent on the potato, especially in the west and southwest.

2. *Characterize the general and specific socio-economic nature of pre-starvation Ireland.*

England's colonial policy was to extract raw materials from its colonies which provided the resources to develop English industry. The impact of this policy on Ireland:

A. Technology was backward:
    1. No significant industry (except in northeast Ireland).
    2. Commerce lagged.
    3. Agricultural technology was primitive and narrow.
    4. Medical technology was grossly deficient, e.g. 39 infirmaries in all Ireland; one for every 366,000 people in Mayo; one for every 6,000 people in Dublin.

B. Social organization:
    1. Early marriage was the rule:
      a. Little chance of accumulating wealth, eliminating any reason to delay marrriage.
      b. Subsistence was possible with some hardship.
      c. However in the two decades prior to the famine, later marriage and greater celibacy were becoming more common.
    2. Land owners were absentee and of a different nationality than the underclass.
    3. Land owners were heavily in debt.
    4. Land owners had to maintain workhouses

in their districts so they often evicted tenants, thus claiming they were not in their district and not liable to provide them even the meager workhouse relief. This created a roving, landless underclass that become easy victims of starvation.

5. Landlords used the one-quarter acre clause to enlarge their holdings as poor, small holders had to part with all land in excess of one-quarter acre in order to qualify for relief.

C. Economic organization:
1. Rents were 80% higher than in England.
2. The 18th century "middlemen systems" allowed extortion and eviction.
3. Evicted peasants had no legal recourse like their English counterparts.
4. Irish properties were treated like modern slum properties, e.g. no improvements, high rents.
5. Most peasants lived outside the cash economy so they couldn't purchase food even if it was available at low cost.
6. Chronic unemployment was characteristic of most of the year.
7. Even in the very best of times, Irish peasants had no hope of finding other work.
8. Until the Tithe Commutation Act of 1838 (p. 52, #11), peasants were obliged to pay a tithe to the Anglican church:
   a. The Commutation Act switched the obligation to pay the tithe to the owner.
   b. Owners in turn raised rents.
9. The right of private property was absolute over the social needs of people about to experience mass starvation.

3. *What was the condition of the following groups on the eve of the Great Starvation?*
A. Irish peasants:
1. Dependent on potato.
2. Producers of food for export.
3. Renting smaller and smaller holdings.
4. Outside the cash economy.
5. Few political rights and power.

6. Public health and medicine primitive.
7. Agricultural technology primitive and narrow.
8. Chronic unemployment for most of the year.
9. A population that had been increasing since the mid-18th century. Ireland was the most densely populated country in Europe.

B. The Irish landlords:
   1. Absentees who were heavily in debt and mortgaged.
   2. Irish properties were treated like modern slum properties, e.g. no improvements, high rents (80% higher than England).
   3. Used middleman system that encouraged exploitation and neglect.
   4. Socially disengaged from and part of a different nationality than the peasant majority.
   5. Often prejudiced towards the peasants due to racism.
   6. Responsible for the poor law rates in their district.
   7. The right of private property was an absolute.

C. British Government:
   1. Laissez-faire political economy that did not allow interference with the market.
   2. Interested in the industrialization of Britain and the prevention of the industrialization of Ireland.
   3. Ireland was treated as a mercantilist colony. It was a:
      a. Source of raw materials.
      b. Source of capital from the profits derived from its land and limited industrial production under English ownership.
      c. Source of labor reserve.
      d. Market for manufactured products.
      e. Producer of cheap food for the British industrial classes.
   4. Ireland was a source of soldiers for colonial armies.

The Great Starvation

1. *What was the bioecological basis of the Great Starvation?*

A. **The beginnings:**
   1. Blight introduced from America in 1845 (phytophora infestans).
   2. After long wet summer the blight appeared first in Waterford and Wexford in September, 1845.
   3. It spread rapidly until half the country was affected.
   4. By August/July, 1846, failure was complete.

B. **Winter 1846-47:**
   1. Was characterized by unusually harsh weather.
   2. Westerly winds failed and cold from Scandanavia and Russia moved into the islands.
   3. Respiratory disease rate was high and contributed to mortality.
   4. Typhus epidemics of 1847 added to the high mortality rate.

C. **1846 - 1848:**
   1. A conservative estimate is that two million people out of a population of nine million were lost to death or migration.
   2. Conservative figures suggest half of those two million people died of starvation or related diseases such as typhus.
   3. Many more left after 1848 as emigration became a way of life for the Irish.
   4. Some place the figure for death or migration as high as three million.

2. *How was the British reaction influenced by political economic theories of private enterprise?*

A. They would not change their laissez-faire policies.

B. No free food could be distributed while private dealers had it for sale.

C. Relief organizations were not allowed to undersell dealers.

D. People of Massachusetts sent a warship full of grain but it was put in storage until the private supply was exhausted.

E. Adherence to such policies, given the history of the Irish peasantry, was in effect genocide.

British Responsibility

1. *Why was government spending inadequate?*

A. They failed to grasp the magnitude of the failure and its potential human impact.

B. Relief was inadequate: seven million pounds was allotted for direct relief and eight million pounds was allotted to purchase maize in 1846-49; but in 1833 they spent twenty million pounds to buy out slave owners in the West Indies and Africa.

C. When Irish crowds gathered to protest the human misery, money was found to send troops to control them.

2. *How did the legal system aid the landlords rather than protect the peasant?*

A. It allowed the landlords to apply to the courts for judgments against tenants in arrears.

B. As soon as a delinquency proceeding was initiated peasants took their belongings and fled because a judgment could mean a prison sentence.
   1. Leaving women and children to shift for themselves.
   2. Leaving the land became a virtual death sentence.

C. This helped get rid of people as the land was immediately cleared.

3. *In 1846 English Prime Minister Peel's abolition of the Corn Laws was supposed to help poor peasants by creating a supply of cheap corn. Why did it fail?*

The Irish had no money to buy any kind of food. They were not part of the cash economy.

A. Peel expected the abolition of the Corn Laws

to innundate United Kingdom markets with cheap foreign corn and thus drive prices down so that the poor could afford to buy it. But foreign corn did not become super abundant and the Irish poor simply had no money to buy it.

B. Grain continued to be exported from Ireland — enough to feed the entire population.

C. Cheap grain prices meant Irish tenants had to produce more grain to pay their rents, driving many thousands to famine.

D. Irish grain bought in England was shipped to Ireland for relief to sell at half price but:
1. Peasants still couldn't afford to buy it.
2. Speculators bought it.
3. Resold it in England to relief agencies, etc.
4. It was then shipped to Ireland again and often bought again by speculators.

4. *What was the nature of the public works programs of 1846-48 and why were they terminated?*

A. People were paid to build useless roads to nowhere, walls, etc. (three million people were dependent on these programs).

B. Many people were too weak to perform.

C. Nothing was spent to develop fisheries, harbors and railroads that would lead to permanent improvement.

D. J. Stuart Mill suggested that the government buy wasteland, turn it to cultivation under peasant proprietorship, but it was never acted upon.

E. The programs were abolished in 1846 then restored and then permanently abolished because they were deemed too expensive.

5. *What was the nature of the soup kitchens?*

A. Public feeding funded by local "poorhouses" or private and church charities, e.g. Quakers.

B. From March 1847 on, the soup kitchen became, along with workhouses, the sole source of aid.

C. Consisted of weak soup and bread, which failed to provide even minimal nutrition.

D. Soup was supplied in some cases to those who would change their religion from Catholic to Protestant.

6. *How did the Poor Law Amendment of 1847 effect the Irish peasant?*

A. It established that no peasant with at least one quarter acre was eligible for relief.

B. Thus, tens of thousands had to give up their land.

C. Those evicted and dispossessed headed for the crowded urban areas where they found workhouses and soup kitchens.

7. *How did prejudice, hostility and racism toward the Irish effect the British approach to the Starvation?*

A. The English considered the Irish an inferior race with an inferior cultural history.

B. By dehumanizing the Irish, it was easier to allow the Irish to die and suffer during the starvation.

C. Press quotes from the period illustrate the English attitude:
   1. *London Times*: called for extermination.
   2. *The Economist*: referred to the Irish as primitive, incompetent, priest-ridden members of an inferior race.
   3. *The Economist*, February 12, 1853: "The departure of the redundant part of the population of Ireland and Scotland is an indispensable preliminary to every kind of 'improvement.'"

D. Political figures such as:
   1. Sir Charles Trevelyan, assistant secretary treasurer, detested the Irish and said "The greatest evil we have to face is not the physical evil of the famine but the moral evil of the selfish, perverse and turbulent character of the people." He liked the fact that the famine encouraged emigration.
   2. Nassau Senior, a prominent economist

and politician wished more would die.
E. The comments of contemporary critics support a thesis of extermination.
 1. Lord Twistleton: resigned in 1849 from the Poor Commission because he viewed it as an "unfit agent for a policy which would be one of extermination."
 2. Lord Clarendon, Lord Lt. of Ireland: "I don't think there is another legislature in Europe that would disregard such suffering as exists in the west of Ireland or coldly persist in a policy of extermination."
F. The English clergy showed little compassion for the Irish, e.g. the Reverend Osborne blamed the reckless improvident breeding of the Irish.

8. *In what ways did the British encourage emigration to the Americas as a solution to the Starvation?*

A. It refused seed potatoes to those who remained thus allowing the starvation to go on longer.

B. Landlords cleared their estates and offered passage to North America for their tenants.

C. Many felt that emigration and death would permanently solve the Irish problem. *The London Times* reported "The Irish are going, going with a vengeance."

D. A rapidly growing Irish population was a threat to English power if militarily organized (Irish growth was twice the English rate).

9. *What evidence exists that could be interpreted as supporting a policy of extermination?*

A. According to some observers, genocide is probable for a government when its representatives knowingly accept mass death as a necessary cost of implementing their policies.

B. The idea of planned mass death is irrelevant. The British government accepted mass death as a part of the price of eliminating the Irish peasantry.

C. Troops were often used to quell unrest and protect food stores.

D. The excuse that Britain accepted the death of its own troops in wartime is different than accepting the death of a conquered nation in peacetime.

10. *Contrast the British, Irish nationalist and Marxist explanations for the genesis of the disaster.*

A. British = due to the basics of Malthusian over-population.

B. Irish nationalists = due to British irresponsibility.

C. Marxists = due to free trade and laissez-faire capitalism that resulted in slave-like social conditions.

The Long Term Effects of the Starvation

1. *What were the effects of the Starvation on Irish agriculture, demography, social organization, Anglo relations?*

A. Agriculture:
   1. Switch to cattle raising.
   2. Reluctance to divide farms.
   3. Less agricultural labor needed.
   4. Evictions were used to clear land, e.g. in Mayo the Earl of Lucan carried out over 40,000 evictions, affecting 306,101 people.
   5. Consolidation of smaller farms, e.g. one to five acre farms totalled 310,436 in 1841, by 1851 the number was reduced to 88,083.
   6. Land was managed so that cattle would thrive while Irish people starved.

B. Demography:
   1. Led to a decline in population growth.
   2. Outflow of poor persons increased between 1845-70. Over three million left.
   3. Population losses by province:
      Leinster = 15.5%
      Ulster = 16.0% (West of the Bann)

Munster = 23.5%
Connaught = 28.5%
4. Institutionalization of emigration as a way of life.
5. The vigorous and young left Ireland.
C. Social organization:
   1. A late transfer of status and postponement of marriage became more common.
   2. An increase in celibacy.
   3. An heir had to wait until father retired to inherit.
D. Anglo relations:
   1. Characterized by distrust and hatred.
   2. It created a major political issue in British politics for the next 70 years.

2. *What were the effects of the Starvation on Irish emigration?*
A. Emigration became a way of life for the young.
B. Those who left and survived:
   1. Convinced others to leave.
   2. Financed the voyages of the others.
C. America was the first choice because:
   1. America made a violent break with England.
   2. More boats were going to America.
   3. Opportunities appeared to be greater in America.

3. *What were the effects of the Starvation on the growth and development of America?*
A. The Irish settled in urban areas and contributed to the growth of urbanization.
B. The Irish supplied the unskilled labor (along with blacks) to build the basis of the industrialization of America e.g. canals, railroads, sewers, water systems, roads, etc.
C. The famine Irish were the most aggressive Catholic group to date, and were willing to challenge Anglo-Americans for their rights.
D. The Irish changed the American Catholic church from a reserved institution to an aggressively growing one and greatly revitalized its parochial school system.

E. The Irish gained control of city politics and developed an urban power base. They didn't invent the "Big City Machine" but they perfected it and this changed the politics of America.

F. The Irish in general became patriotic Americans and willingly staffed armies and supported American expansion.

G. The memory of the famine formed the basis for a deep, enduring hatred of England and fueled Irish-American support for Irish freedom fighters.

For Further Reading and Study

Connell, K. 1962. *The Potato in Irish History. Past and Present.* 23:57-71.

Gallagher, T. 1982. *Paddy's Lament.* Harcourt, Brace and Janovich, NY.

Gibbon, P. 1975. *Colonialism and the Great Starvation in Ireland, 1845-49.* Race and Class. 17:2:321-336.

Lees, .H. and J.H. Modell. 1977. *The Irish Countryman Urbanized: A Comparative Perspective on the Migration.* Journal of Urban History. 3:4:391-408.

Mokyr, J. and C. O'Grada. 1982. *Emigration and Poverty in Pre-Famine Ireland.* Explorations in Economic History. 19:4:360-384.

Rubenstein, R.L. 1983. *The Irish Famine.* In: *The Age of Triage.* R.L. Rubenstein. Beacon Press, Boston. pp. 98-127.

Woodham-Smith, C. 1972. *The Great Hunger.* Harper and Row, NY.

CHAPTER NINE

The Fenians to the fall of Parnell

1850-1897

The Fenian Legacy

1. What were the major factors that led to the rise of the Fenian movement in the mid 19th century?

A. The working conditions of the laboring classes in mid 19th century Ireland were characterized by:
 1. Long hours.
 2. Unhealthy surroundings.
 3. Low wages.

B. The Irish and British working classes were struggling and agitating against industrial exploitation.

C. The price of necessities such as food, clothing, and rent had doubled from the 1850's to the 1860's.

D. Irish industrial progress was being sacrificed to keep the Irish producing cheap food for the British laboring classes, except in Ulster where industrialization was encouraged.

2. _The Fenian movement broadly consisted of the following organizations:_

A. **The Phoenix Society:** a secret society formed by a federation of the left-overs from the Irish Confederation (p. 54, #17 & #19) and Repeal Association (p. 52, #12) in the region of West Cork and Kerry. It was founded in 1856 under the influence of Jeremiah O'Donovan Rossa who believed that the well-being of Ireland rested in ousting the British. In 1857 after a visit from James Stephens, a former Young Irelander who suggested the possibility of a trans-Atlantic revolutionary movement, they began to drill and arm. The Phoenix Society eventually evolved into the IRB and its American branch, the Fenian Brotherhood.

B. **IRB:** the Irish Republican Brotherhood or Irish Revolutionary Brotherhood, was a secret society founded in Dublin in 1858 that vowed to use physical force to free Ireland from British rule. James Stephens and O'Donovan Rossa were the principle founders. An attempt was made to establish a fifth column within the British Army.

C. **Fenian Brotherhood:** a secret society founded in New York in 1858 simultaneously with the founding of the IRB in Dublin. It was the American wing of the IRB. It was founded by Michael Doheny and John O'Mahoney by converting a group founded in 1856, the Emmet Memorial Association, into the Fenian Brotherhood.

D. *The Irish People:* the official newspaper of the Fenian Movement founded in Dublin on November 29, 1863. It was edited by Thomas Clarke Luby and John O'Leary with O'Donovan Rossa as business manager. It was attacked by the priests and employers, but its circulation grew. On September 15, 1865, the British arrested many Fenian leaders including Luby, O'Leary and Rossa. They were tried, convicted and sentenced to 25 years to life at penal servitude.

3. *What were the major problems associated with the Fenian Movement?*

A. Catholic Church in Ireland opposed it because:

   1. It threatened Cardinal Cullen's own political organization, the National Association. The National Association was founded in 1864 to promote Catholic middle class causes in the House of Commons such as tenant rights, denominational education and disestablishment of the Protestant church. It included John Blake Dillon, Myles O'Reilly and John Francis

McQuire. The tenant rights part
of the platform was probably included
as a ploy to attract broader support for
the more sectarian aspects of the
Association.
2. It was thought to be related to the anti-
clerical nationalism on the continent based
on the model of Garibaldi in Italy.
B. The spirit of the people was very low in the
aftermath of the famine 1845-1851.
C. Privileged groups in Ireland were especially
opposed to it.
D. Urban middle class and better-off tenant farmers opposed it because their well-being was
tied to Britain's presence.

4. *How did the Terrence McManus funeral become a power play between the republicans
and Cardinal Cullen?*
A. In December 1860, Terrence McManus, an
exiled Young Irelander, died in California.
B. The Fenians decided to send his body back to
Ireland for burial.
   1. It was carried by train across the United
   States.
   2. Stops were made for viewing in areas
   where Irish-American populations
   requested it .
   3. The body did not leave for Ireland until
   September 1861.
C. In Ireland:
   1. Cardinal Cullen refused to bury him from
   the Catholic Church.
   2. The IRB waked him at Mechanics
   Institute (later the Abbey Theater).
      a. 50,000 to 100,000 followed the coffin
      to Glasnevin Cemetary in Dublin on
      November 10, 1861.
      b. A Mayo priest, Patrick Lavelle, buried
      him.
      c. A halt was made at every spot sacred
      in the revolutionary history of Ire-
      land e.g. the house where Robert
      Emmet (pp. 45-46, #6 & #7) was hung;
      the house that held Wolfe Tone's body

before burial; the house where Lord Edward Fitzgerald (p. 41, #5.D) was wounded in 1798.

3. It was a great psychological victory over the church hierarchy.

5. *In what ways was the American Civil War used to prepare for revolution in Ireland?*

A. Irish Americans supported the union in order to keep America strong in relationship to Britain.

B. They also saw it as a training ground for an Irish revolution and possibly up to 200,000 were sworn into the Fenian Brotherhood.

6. *What was the outcome of the Fenians Civil War training strategy?*

A. After the war the Fenians included about 50,000 veterans within their ranks.

B. But the Fenians were wracked by dissension and factionalism and split into two major factions:

1. Colonel William Roberts faction wanted to attack British imperialism in Canada.

2. The O'Mahoney/Stephens/Devoy faction wanted to send money, arms and men to Ireland.

C. The Roberts Faction invaded Canada in May of 1866.

1. They were using U.S. army surplus equipment.

2. The U.S. used the Fenians as a threat for leverage in their negotiations with the British on:

a. The Alabama claims dispute.

b. The recognition of naturalized U.S. citizens.

3. The initial invasion met with some success but ran short of supplies and was defeated.

4. Two other attempts at later dates in Vermont and the prairie provinces also failed.

7. **What was the nature of the Fenian insurrection in Ireland in 1867?**
A. Risings occurred in Kerry, Cork, Tipperary, Limerick, Dublin, Clare, etc. during February and March of 1867.
B. They largely attacked RIC (Royal Irish Constabulary) barracks.
C. The Fenians failed militarily because:
   1. The movement had been infiltrated by British spies.
   2. It was poorly timed; actually postponed and rescheduled from February to March.
   3. Many of the major leaders were in jail or on the run.
   4. Unseasonably fierce weather conditions in Ireland.

8. **How did the case of the Manchester Martyrs affect the Fenian Movement?**
A. On September 18, 1867 a group of Fenians attacked a prison van in order to free two of their leaders, Tom Kelly and Tim Deasy.
B. In blowing open the van a police sergeant was accidentally killed.
C. William Allen, Michael Larkin and Michael O'Brien were tried and convicted of murder, although none were guilty and one may not have even been present.
D. They were executed on November 23, 1867, in Manchester, England (only the hanging of John Brown after Harper's Ferry was similar).
E. The hanging united the Irish people in support of the Fenians:
   1. Even the church softened.
   2. "God Save Ireland," a song written about the three, became an unofficial national anthem of Ireland.
F. Another explosion, wrongly attributed to the Fenians in Clerkenwell England on December 13, 1867, hurt growing support for the Fenians in England.
G. In 1870, under pressure from the British, the pope condemned the Fenians (IRB) but the Irish people did not like it.

H. In 1869 O'Donovan Rossa was elected to Parliament from Tipperary while imprisoned for Fenianism.
   1. He refused to wear a prison uniform.
   2. He wanted recognition as a political prisoner.
   3. Parliament disqualified him from office.
   4. Tipperary then elected another recently released Fenian.

9. *What is the legacy of the Fenian Movement?*
A. It resurrected the non-sectarian ideals of the United Irishmen (pp. 38-39, #1, #2).
B. Re-established the right of the Irish people to use force to gain their freedom.
C. Even to this day the term Fenian evokes hate from British loyalists:
   1. Considered a vile epithet.
   2. Gradually extended to include all Irish Catholics regardless of political affiliation.
   3. Today on the Shankhill Road in Belfast loyalists refer to nationalists as "Fenian bastards."

10. *What was the real nature of the Fenian movement?*
A. It was based on the theory of Auguste Blanqui, a French revolutionary who developed the concept of the secret conspiratorial brotherhood in the 1830s and 40s. The Fenians adopted the notion of a pledge-bound, hand-picked, disciplined elite who would act as the shock troops of the revolution.
B. It was a physical force tradition that rejected constitutional nationalism.
C. It was hostile to sectarianism and clericalism believing in strict separation of church and state.
D. It was democratic, republican and socialistic (advocating the expropriation of landlords as a class).
E. It was the first national movement that was largely based on the underclasses: small farm-

ers, laborers, clerks, shop assistants, etc.

F. It wrote-off the landed aristocracy and urban middle class as anti-revolutionary because of their ties with Britain.

G. Its primary goal was complete independence.

H. It also supported a Gaelic revival.

11. How did the Fenians influence Prime Minister Gladstone (1868-1984)?

A. The demonstration of national spirit awakened him to the real importance of the Irish question.

B. His first administration sought to solve the Irish problems:
1. Church Act of 1869: de-established and disendowed the Church of Ireland.
2. Land Act of 1870: the first attempt to provide land reforms for tenants, but it proved ineffective because landlords simply wouldn't abide by it.
3. University Bill of 1873: attempted to establish a great new University of Dublin with branches throughout the country, but it too failed due to opposition from special interests.

12. What was the Clan na Gael and what were its objectives?

A. It was a secret society founded by Jerome Collins in the United States in 1867.

B. Its major objectives were the liberation of Ireland from British rule and the promotion of Irish culture. Their activities centered around raising funds and weapons for Irish independence.

C. It was more secret than the Fenians in order to prevent the spy infiltration that characterized the Fenians.

D. From 1871 on, John Devoy, a former Fenian, came to dominate it.

E. In 1877 they formed an alliance with the IRB and established a joint directory to free Ireland.

F. It attracted many prominent Americans such as T.V. Powderly of the Knights of Labor.

G. Between 1876-1881, the Clan funded County Clare man John Holland for his research on the submarine, providing him $60,000, with the idea of using this technology to attack British ships. Holland called his submarine the "Fenian Ram."

The Struggle for Home Rule

1. *Discuss the role of Isaac Butt in the struggle for home rule.*

A. In 1870 he founded the Home Government Association.

B. He proposed a federation of Ireland and Britain in a booklet, *Irish Federalism* in 1870.

C. It would have featured a subordinate parliament with direct control over Irish domestic affairs.

D. He organized the Irish Parliamentary Party in 1874 which later came to be known simply as The Irish Party. The Party was an advocate of Irish Home Rule, or self-government within th British empire.

E. In the election of 1874, the first fought under the Ballot Act of 1872 (secret voting), the Party won half the Irish seats.

2. *Why did Butt's approach fail?*

A. His call for home rule was not taken seriously by Britain.

B. His ideas of confederation fell far short of the independence favored by many of his allies.

C. A small group within his party began to call for a policy of obstructionism to advance the cause of Irish issues.

D. He bent over backwards to appease the British government in order to win their respect and confidence.

3. *How was obstructionism used to foster Irish issues?*

A. Irish Party Members of Parliament Joseph Biggar and John Power obstructed debate in Parliament on important British issues in order to highlight the Irish question.

B. They were joined in 1875 by Charles Parnell, who further developed the tactic in order to force action on Irish issues.

C. Parnell was elected head of The Irish Party in 1880.

4. *Who was Charles S. Parnell (1846-1891)?*

Born in Wicklow, Charles Parnell came from a landowning Protestant family. He was elected to Parliament in 1875 and quickly rose to prominence as an advocate of Irish Home Rule. He was elected head of the Irish Party in 1880.

At the urging of Michael Davitt (p. 80, #7) Parnell became an advocate of land reform and president of the National Land League. He was a firebrand, and Fenian leader Charles Kickham once remarked that the Irish people "would go to the gates of hell" for the land and Parnell.

5. *What were the conditions in Ireland that led to an alliance between the Clan na Gael and the Irish Party?*

A. In the winter of 1878-79, the rural population of Ireland was threatened with disaster similar to that of the Great Famine.

B. Falling prices, crop failures and wet weather were leading to bankruptcy, starvation and eviction of small farmers.

C. Irish Party leader Charles Parnell understood the land question was a key ingredient in arousing the passions of the Irish masses and so adapted land reform to harness this momentum for change. Clan na Gael and the IRB also saw land reform agitation as an appropriate vehicle for encouraging mass revolt against the British.

6. **What was the New Departure policy?**

A. Michael Davitt of the Land League (p. 80, # 7) travelled to America and met with John Devoy and others in Clan na Gael who wanted a link with the Irish masses.

B. They formulated the New Departure Plan:
    1. Parnellites would keep arguing for home rule.
    2. While Clan na Gael and the IRB would prepare for revolution.
    3. The Clan and IRB recruited and radicalized the masses by campaigning for:
        a. Fair rent agitation.
        b. Tenants' right to sell their interest if they were evicted.
        c. Complete abolition of the landlord system.
        d. Establishment of a peasant proprietorship.
    4. Parnell would eventually call for home rule by 1882 and when the British refused a revolt would be initiated.

7. **What was the National Land League and what were its major objectives?**

A. An organization founded by Michael Davitt known as the Mayo Land League in 1879.

B. It shortly became the National Land League, with Parnell taking Davitt's place as head.

C. It demanded the end of the landlord system.

D. It advocated the three F's:
    1. **Fair rent** based on the value of the land, instead of the inflated rates the landlords demanded.
    2. **Fixity of tenure** so tenants would not arbitrarily be ejected from the land.
    3. **Free sale of the tenancy** so tenants who left the land would receive compensation for the improvements they made.

E. It used the boycott and rent withholding.

F. It enlisted massive support.

G. In America a Clan na Gael front, the Irish National and Industrial League, collected money to fund the League's activities.

H. American money funded the League:

    1. To aid evicted tenants.

    2. To purchase legal aid for farmers.

8. What was the Land War?

A. A period of massive resistance to landlordism between 1879-1882.

B. It consisted of an elaborate system of moral force warfare.

    1. Embargoes placed on evicted farms; nothing could move in or out of them.

    2. Families evicted for non-payment were sheltered and supported.

    3. Families of those sent to prison were cared for.

    4. Those prosecuted were defended by the Land League.

    5. The boycott was used to socially ostracize collaborators.

    6. Process-serving and evictions were accompanied by huge demonstrations.

C. The old secret society traditions introduced some violence toward landlords, e.g. Ribbonmen.

D. The Land League sanctions were more effective than the government; an alternative rural government nearly existed.

E. "Ulster Custom" (see Ulster Tenant Right, p. 23 #1.D) which guaranteed the 3-F's to loyalist tenants largely exempted Ulster from the Land War.

9. How did American groups aid in the Land War?

A. American money funded it:

    1. To aid evicted tenants.

    2. To purchase legal aid for tenants.

B. Americans publicized the anti-landlord case abroad.

10. What was the nature of Parnell's and English Prime Minister Gladstone's cooperation?

A. Parnell switched from obstructionism to balance of power politics.

B. In 1880 a home rule bill failed.

C. An 1881 Land Act guaranteed farmers stable tenure at a fair rent, which destroyed the landlord system in Ireland.

D. Parnell wanted the Land Act to include those tenants in arrears and opposed it.

11. *Identify the Kilmainham "Treaty."*

A. After they opposed the Land Act in 1881 the Irish Party leaders, including Parnell, were arrested and jailed.

B. In March 1882, Gladstone visited Parnell in Kilmainham Jail and reached an agreement to support a modified land act.

C. Government coercion was to cease and arrears would be taken care of by Gladstone.

D. The prisoners were released and the Land War ended.

E. But some wanted open insurrection.

12. *Why was the Irish Parliamentary Party under Parnell said to be the most effective party in the British Parliament?*

A. It brought the grievances of the Irish home to the British people as no other group had.

B. It cooperated with the Liberal Party and achieved some definite changes.

C. It made the Irish issue a major part of British politics — governments fell because of it.

13. *How did Parnell fall from power?*

A. Captain O'Shea named him in his divorce from Kitty O'Shea, as Parnell had been having an affair with her for many years.

B. Gladstone and the Liberals said Parnell had to go as a leader, at least for awhile.

C. The Catholic church, the British press and the Tories attacked Parnell's morals and fitness for public office.

D. Parnell refused to quit, but the Irish Party replaced him with Justin McCarthy.

E. Parnell took his case to the people and travelled the countyside making speeches.

F. He died of the strains on October 6, 1891, at 45 years of age.

For Further Reading and Study

Bew, P. 1979. *Land and the National Question in Ireland 1858-1882*. Humanities Press. Atlantic Highlands, NJ.

Davitt, M. 1904. *The Fall of Feudalism in Ireland* or *The Story of the Land League Revolution*. Harper, New York.

Jackson, T.W. 1970. *Ireland Her Own*. Chapters 13, 14, 15, 16, and 17. International Publishers, New York.

Larkin, E. 1979. *The Roman Catholic Church in Ireland and the Fall of Parnell, 1888-91*. Univ. North Carolina, Chapel Hill.

Moody, T.W., ed. 1968. *The Fenian Movement*. Mercier, Cork.

_____. 1981. *Davitt and the Irish Revolution, 1841-1882*. Oxford Univ., Oxford.

_____. 1984. *Fenianism, Home Rule and the Land War (1850-1890)*. In: *The Course of Irish History*. T.W. Moody and F.X. Martin,eds. Mercier, Cork. pp. 275-293.

Newsinger, J. 1982. *A Great Blow Must Be Struck in Ireland: Karl Marx and the Fenians*. Race and Class. 24:2:151-167.

CHAPTER TEN

From the fall of Parnell to the Civil War and its after effects   1891 – 1949

1. Why was the Irish Party less effective after the fall of Parnell?

A. Personality differences between John Dillon, Tim Healy and William O'Brien led to feuding within the Party.

B. Strategy differences developed, especially the attempt by Healy to restructure the Party to give the clergy a prominent role, leading to a drift toward sectarianism.

C. British liberals were reevaluating their Irish alliance, since many members thought the home rule issue was alienating the Party from the British electorate.

D. The Irish Party's sympathy for the Boers in 1899-1902 was considered unpatriotic by the British.

E. Supporters in the United States were less enthusiastic about the Party after the fall of Parnell, resulting in a shortage of funds coming from America.

2. How did the revitalization of the Irish Party under John Redmond affect funding from the United States?

A. The United Irish League of America was founded in 1901 to support Redmond. Redmond represented a moderate element in favor of Home Rule.

B. American money came to pay the allowance for one-half the Irish Party until 1911.

C. American money covered most of the Party's election expenses in 1906 and 1910.

3. **What was the Gaelic League and how did it influence Irish nationalism?**

A. It was an organization founded on July 31, 1893, in Dublin by Douglas Hyde, Eoin McNeill, Eugene O'Growney and others.

B. Its aim was the revival of the Gaelic language as well as Gaelic music, and crafts.

C. It set up over 400 branches and published pamphlets and text books on Gaelic language and culture.

D. It stimulated the teaching of Irish in national schools and by 1913 Irish became a compulsory subject at the National University.

E. The work of the League inspired many young people to be proud of their Irish heritage.

F. Its greatest strength was in the towns and among young people, the peasantry was in general indifferent.

G. It was actively opposed by :
   1. The British establishment.
   2. The Catholic church, who primarily opposed the physical force proponents within the Gaelic League.

H. By 1915, Sinn Fein activists took it over and made it as much a political as a cultural organization.

I. On November 25, 1919, the League was suppressed for defiance of British authority.

J. Padraic Pearse called it "the most revolutionary influence that has ever come into Irish history."

4. **What was the Gaelic Atheletic Association (GAA)?**

The Gaelic Athletic Association (GAA) was founded in 1884 — nine years before the Gaelic League — to promote traditional Irish sports. It worked hand in hand with the Gaelic League and also contained nationalistic elements. GAA chapters still exist today in Ireland and in many parts of the world, including the United States.

5. *What was the importance of the agricultural cooperatives founded by Horace Plunkett in 1893?*

A. He wanted to modernize Irish agriculture with production and distribution co-operatives modeled on Denmark.

B. Its success was illustrated by the great number of cooperative creameries that were established. They were eventually destroyed by the British in the War of Independence (1919-21) in order to cripple the Irish economy.

6. *How did the Boer War (1899 – 1902), in which the British waged a savage battle for control of southern African natural resources, influence Irish American politics with respect to British rule in Ireland?*

A. Irish Americans denounced the war:
   1. Organized mass meetings.
   2. Some even sent volunteers to fight with the Boers.

B. Clan na Gael became revitalized in 1900:
   1. Publicly attacked an alleged secret alliance of the USA with Britain.
   2. President McKinley offered his assistance in ending the war since he feared alliance of Irish-Americans, German-Americans and anti-imperialists.

C. Even the United Irish Society, a Chicago-based coalition of Irish organizations, agitated against the war and sent 500 volunteers. They became involved because they saw it as an opportunity to strike against England.

D. Both the Republican and Democratic Parties had to carry planks in 1900 denouncing the Boer War.

7. *In what ways did Irish-Americans influence Anglo-American relations in the early 20th century?*

A. An Irish-American/German-American alliance prevented the United States from supporting Britain in its attempts to limit German and Russian expansion in the Far East.

B. John Hay, Secretary of State, admitted in 1905 that the Clan na Gael and their allies helped to defeat three of four Anglo-United States treaties between 1897-1917.

C. In 1900 the Clan na Gael began to publicize the Indian nationalist cause against Britain.

D. The Ancient Order of Hibernians (AOH) and the German-American Alliance entered into a formal agreement to cooperate on issues relating to British influence around the world.

8. *How did Redmond's stand on World War I influence his support in the United States?*

A. Redmond agreed to support the war in hopes of being rewarded with home rule after the war.

B. It angered nationalists and destroyed the United Irish League of America which supported Redmond's Irish Party.

C. The Clan na Gael wanted the United States to remain neutral while the AOH supported the Germans.

D. The British government had to work actively in the United States to counter Irish-American opposition to the war.

E. The pro-British United States government and media conducted campaigns against hyphenated Americans.

9. *What was the role of Edward Carson in the Home Rule issue?*

A. A unionist Member of Parliament from Dublin who not only opposed home rule, but every other piece of liberal legislation from old age pensions to social insurance.

B. He was not only against home rule for Ulster but all of Ireland.

C. He was an anti-Catholic racist who viewed Irish Catholics as inferior.

D. He deliberately fomented religious discord and made threats of physical violence in an effort to derail home rule.

E. In 1912, he signed a covenant with other leaders to use all means necessary to defeat home rule.

F. He encouraged the founding of the Ulster Volunteer Force (UVF) to militarily resist home rule.

G. He also opposed partition because he wanted all of Ireland to remain under British rule.

10. What were the main points of Arthur Griffith's philosophy in the early 20th century that he used to develop the Sinn Fein Party?

A. The Irish people should use only Irish manufactured goods.

B. This would stimulate the development of a Irish national economy.

C. Members of Parliament should withdraw from Westminster to form an Irish National Council to promote further Irish manufacturing growth and secure trade abroad.

D. This sort of self-help policy would bring capital to Ireland and stop emigration.

E. It would then lead to the forced restoration of an Irish Parliament on the model of "Grattan's Parliament" of 1782-1800 (p. 38, #3).

F. It also promoted cultural separatism.

11. Why did Arthur Griffith propose a dual monarchy?

A. He thought that Ireland didn't have the military strength to break the British connection.

B. He felt it was a compromise between home rule and republicanism that would persuade Britain to grant an Irish Parliament.

C. It was to be modeled on that of the Austro-Hungarian empire.

Organizing and carrying out the 1916 Rising

1. How was the Irish Republican Brotherhood (IRB) revived in the early 1900s?

A. At the turn of the century new leaders like Thomas J. Clarke, Bullmer Hobson and Sean

McDermott gave the movement a boost.

B. The IRB infiltrated the Gaelic League, the Gaelic Athletic Association and later Sinn Fein.

C. By 1910 the IRB was publishing a paper, *Irish Freedom*.

D. With England's attention focussed on World War I, the IRB Supreme Council secretly developed plans for a rising to take place in 1916, utilizing the armed Irish Volunteers (formed in 1913 to defend Home Rule efforts) and the Irish Citizen Army.

2. *How did the militancy of Irish trade unions contribute to the struggle for freedom?*

A. Worker militancy lead by James Larkin and James Connolly from 1913 on brought massive rallies, baton charges by the RIC, riots, arrests, imprisonments and a few deaths.

B. The Irish Citizen Army was established as a workers defense organization during the Great Dublin Lockout in 1913. James Connolly, a labor and revolutionary leader, revived the force after the labor unrest ended to play an important part in the Easter Rising of 1916.

C. The Irish Socialist Republican Party founded by Connolly in 1896 expounded both socialist and nationalist objectives for Ireland.

3. *What was the 1916 Easter Rising and its significance in Irish history?*

A. On Easter Monday, 1916, the Irish Volunteers and the Citizen Army seized control of key areas in Dublin city.

B. Padraic Pearse, president of the provisional Republic, publicly read a Proclamation declaring the independence of Ireland.

C. The rebellion was largely confined to Dublin because Eoin McNeill, Volunteer Commander, discovered that a rebellion, not a practice maneuver was afoot, and issued orders cancelling the maneuvers.

D. Between 1,500 and 2,000 took part, including 50 members of the Hibernian Rifles from America and over 50 women.

E. Outside Dublin some groups did rise briefly, e.g. Liam Mellows captured Athenry in county Galway.

4. How did the Proclamation of 1916 show a fusion of Pearse's ideas with those of James Connolly?

A. The part that declared "the right of the peoples of Ireland to ownership of Ireland" comes from both James Connolly and James Fintan Lalor.

B. At the same time it pledged their lives to Irish freedom and Ireland's exaltation among nations. This seems to follow Pearse's idea of a blood sacrifice necessary to revitalize the Irish people.

C. In *The Sovereign People* pamphlet Pearse called for the ownership and possession of Irish soil for all its people, not just the rich.

5. What was the role of the Clan na Gael in the Easter Rising of 1916?

A. It provided partial funding, including the purchase of weapons.

B. They were involved in the planning and were the only American group to know of it ahead of time.

6. How did British treatment of the rebel prisoners shift public opinions?

A. The brutal repression turned both the Irish people and Americans toward the rebels.

B. Ninety rebels were sentenced to death, and over a period of a few weeks in May, 1916, the slow, deliberate executions of the leaders shocked even conservative clergymen. James Connolly, too ill to stand because of infected wounds sustained during the Rising, was tied to a chair and shot.

C. Great Britain was actually worried that the United States might break the blockade of the Central Powers.

D. The shift of public sentiment, especially in Dublin, turned the rebels into martyrs and national heroes.

E. The bravery of the rebels reawakened dormant ideas of nationhood and started a movement that eventually culminated in the Anglo-Irish War (1919-21) and nominal independence for 26 of the Ireland's counties.

After the Rising: build-up to the Anglo-Irish War

1. How did Sinn Fein change from the original ideas of Arthur Griffith after the Easter Rising?

In 1917 Sinn Fein underwent a reorganization that included a new constitution and the election of the only surviving commandant of the Easter Rising, Eamon DeValera, as its President. The character of the Party became decidely republican, and supportive of the armed volunteers.

2. How did the Parliamentary election of 1918 highlight the desires of the majority of the Irish people for independence?

A. Sinn Fein won 73 seats to 6 for home rulers and 26 for the unionists (36 of Sinn Feiners were in jail and many were on the run).

B. Two-thirds of all voters in Ireland chose republicanism and they controlled 29 of the counties.

C. Only in small sections of the northeast did the unionists gain control.

D. Sinn Fein ran on a platform of separation from Britain.

3. What was the response of Sinn Fein to its overwhelming victory?

A. They refused to take their seats at Westminster in protest of British rule over Ireland.

B. They assembled in Dublin as the first Dail Eireann and began to rule Ireland in the name of Irish Republic.

C. They established arbitration courts to replace the British system, and Industrial Disputes Board to mediate labor disputes, a Land Bank to offer land purchase loans.

D. They attempted to send representatives to the Versailles Peace Conference, but were not admitted.

4. *What was the British response to Sinn Fein?*

A. The Dail Eireann and associated agencies were declared illegal assemblies.

B. Britain embarked upon the Anglo-Irish War in an effort to militarily crush the rebellion (1919-21).

C. The Irish Volunteers, now known as the Irish Republican Army (IRA), acted to protect the Dail and the newly declared Republic against British aggression.

5. *What is the significance of DeValera's trip to America in 1919?*

A. He sold Irish Bond Certificates redeemable after independence.

B. American Commission on Conditions in Ireland and the American Commission for Relief in Ireland collected over $5,000,000.

C. A bitter split developed between DeValera and some Irish Americans led by Judge Cohalan because Cohalan was spending money from the Irish Victory Fund to defeat the League of Nations rather than in Ireland.

D. The trip raised American consciousness with respect to the Anglo-Irish War.

6. *What was the nature and progress of the Anglo-Irish War (1919-21)?*

A. Britain, determined to crush the independent Dail Eireann, used spies, informers and the Royal Irish Constabulary (RIC) in attempts to crush the movement. In March of 1920 they introduced an element of terrorism in the form of the Black and Tans. Recruits for the Black and Tans were picked from among violent criminal offenders. Prison sentences were pardoned if the criminals volunteered for service. The Black and Tans used murder, arson, torture, rape and systematic beating up and looting of whole areas.

B. The IRA carried out a guerilla war with hit and run tactics (flying columns) that included attacks on barracks, ambushes of crown forces and arms raids.

C. The IRA with the support of the people developed into an effective force under Michael Collins that paralyzed and defeated British forces throughout Ireland.

D. Republican courts were established and accepted by the people and decisions were enforced by Republican Police (IRA).

E. However, by the end of the war the Black and Tan losses were so high that they virtually retreated to their barracks in many areas.

7. Identify: Black and Tans and IRA.

A. **Black and Tans**— a force sent to Ireland by Britain that had a social composition similar to the Nazis SS troops; in fact Hitler and Mussolini copied the concept. The name is a result of the fact that they wore uniforms that were a mixture of dark and khaki colors.

B. **IRA**— the Irish Republican Army, a guerilla force or people's army that fought to liberate Ireland from British rule. (pp. 103-104, #5-#7)

8. How did U.S. President Woodrow Wilson view the Irish cause and its Irish-American supporters?

A. Wilson disliked Irish-Americans:
   1. He thought they were disloyal because many Irish Americans saw World War I as an opportunity to strike against England.
   2. He was an anti-Catholic bigot.
   3. He personally hated Judge Cohalan, one of the major Irish American leaders.

B. He said that self-determination only included lands formerly held by the Central Powers (World War I).

C. He needed Britain's help to form the League

of Nations, therefore he wouldn't help Ireland.

9. How did Irish-Americans react to Wilson's attitude?

A. Clan na Gael and its front, the Friends of Irish Freedom, launched a campaign against the League of Nations. It was simply an effort to deny Wilson's dream of a League because he refused to help Ireland.

B. They were led by Judge Cohalan, a prominent Irish American judge from New York.

C. Their approach included:
   1. Large mass protest meetings.
   2. Taking out full page newspaper ads where ever Wilson traveled.
   3. Making alliances with their traditional opponents such as Senators Lodge and Borah.

D. They helped to stop America's entry into the League of Nations.

10. Who was Terence MacSwiney and what was his impact on the on the Anglo-Irish conflict?

He was the Lord Mayor of Cork and an IRA man who died on October 25, 1920, in Brixton Prison, England, after a 74-day hunger strike. Arrested by British forces for conducting a meeting at the Cork City Hall, he embarked on the hunger strike to protest his illegal imprisonment and the British presence in Ireland. A massive funeral, "one that a king might envy," was held after his death. The world was shocked by British intransigence, and tremendous public and diplomatic pressure was exerted on the British government to end the war in Ireland.

Birth of Northern Ireland and the Irish Civil War (1922-23)

1. How did the entity of Northern Ireland come into existence?

Unable to defeat the Irish militarily in the Anglo-

Irish War, English Prime Minister Lloyd George was determined to thwart the movement for Irish independence. Possibly, the British felt that they could not afford to lose Ireland as they feared revolts in other parts of the Empire such as India. Lloyd George opened negotiations with representatives of the Provisional Irish government in 1921, offering home rule for the 26 counties — an Irish Free State under the authority of the British Crown — while six counties (Northern Ireland) would remain temporarily under Britain. Irish Free State officials would be bound by an Oath of Allegiance to the Crown.

This offer was made under the threat of accelerating the Anglo-Irish war to a devastating level, including the aerial bombing of Irish cities if the offer had been rejected. The inexperienced Irish negotiators accepted and signed the treaty on December 6, 1921.

After a heated debate in the Dail Eireann, the treaty was approved by a vote of 64-57 on January 7, 1922. All the female representatives in the Dail, including Mary MacSwiney, voted against it. A bloody civil war broke out between "republicans" who rejected the treaty and "Free Staters" who accepted it.

2. *Why was the oath of allegiance a critical issue in the Anglo-Irish negotiations?*

A. If the Irish accepted dominion status they would be forced to take an oath of allegiance to the British crown.

B. The Irish refused to accept such an oath and countered with DeValera's idea of external association (see D below).

C. The British, however, had a strong emotional attachment to the monarchy as a symbol of British history, culture, and political dominance.

D. External association consisted of the Irish Republic recognizing the crown as the head of an association of independent states known as the British Commonwealth — but with no oath of allegiance to a foreign monarch.

E. The argument over the oath distracted many

republicans from the issue of partition, which was ultimately more important than an oath.

3. *Why did the British want to remain in part of Ireland?*
A. For military/defensive reasons.
B. To allow the British to maintain direct and indirect control over all of Ireland.
C. To protect capitalist investment which was concentrated in the northeast.
D. To preserve British prestige.
E. To satisfy a loyalist (p. 139 #2) majority concentrated in one and one-half counties.

4. *What was the Irish Civil War (1922-1923) and what was its significance?*

It was a war that erupted between republican anti-treaty forces and Free State pro-treaty forces. The Free Staters were supported by the British while the IRA split, joining both sides. It divided families and created many lasting emotional wounds among the Irish people.

It was a bloody confrontation in which many of Ireland's most promising political and social leaders died. The republican forces were defeated but went underground in order to carry on the fight for an undivided republic. The Irish Civil War was a period in which deep political divisions were born, and many of those divisions still resound in today's divided Irish political scene.

5. *What was the reaction of Irish-Americans to the Irish Civil War?*
A. Most Irish-Americans accepted the treaty as the best that could be achieved.
B. Many Irish-Americans never really understood the differences between Home Rule, Dominion Status, External Association, a Republic, etc.
C. The civil war left most Irish Americans:
   1. Confused.
   2. Disgusted.
   3. Turned off.

D. But small groups of well-informed Irish-Americans, lead by individuals such as Joe McGarrity, did not accept the treaty and supported the various campaigns to free the six counties.

6. *What are the fallacies associated with the revisionist view of the history of the Easter Rising through the Civil War?*

A. Revisionists claim that the British would eventually have granted home rule or dominion status as British public opinion changed in the post-colonial era.

B. They feel that the blood shed was unnecessary and has led to the cult of the gunmen today.

C. But they neglect to consider that it was in Ireland, the first of Britain's colonies, that the whole empire began to crumble —Nehru in India and others observed the Irish example.

D. They ignore the history of colonial struggles for freedom where armed struggle or the threat of armed struggle was the most important ingredient in the achievement of independence.

E. They ignore the role of the folklore or the popular culture history of patriotism as a driving force in a people's cultural history.

7. *What was the Boundary Commission of 1925 and in what ways was it biased toward partition?*

A. A group appointed by Lloyd George to re-evaluate the geographic dimensions of the original boundary between the six counties and the Irish Free State. Nationalists were led to believe that the Commission would relocate the boundary and hand over additional land with nationalist majorities in the counties of Fermanagh, Tyrone, Armagh and Down to the Irish Free State.

B. In 1924 the Commission met with Justice R. Feetham of South Africa as chair.

C. The Commission proceeded to use a loophole

in the Treaty of 1921-22 (Article XII) to maintain the boundary as it was based on it being "compatible with economic and geographical conditions."

D. McNeill, the Free State member, resigned.

E. Amid rumors of actually expanding the six-county state —the Free State government accepted the frontier in December 1925. W. T. Cosgrove, signing for the Free State government, was promised a cancellation of Irish war debts to England. He called the agreement, "a damned good bargain."

8. What were Ireland's major problems after the Civil War?

A. A legacy of hatred led to the factionalization of Irish politics.

B. Ireland was an underdeveloped country with respect to natural resources, agriculture and industry.

C. Partition deprived the new state of its most industrialized section, the northeast.

D. The new state was overly dependent on Britain with respect to trade. Ninety percent of Ireland's imports/exports were with Britain.

E. Irish agriculture was in general inefficient and lacking appropriate technology to compete in the world market.

F. Domestic industries were inefficient and unemployment was high.

G. Emigration deprived the country of a lot of youthful talent.

H. The hierarchy of the Catholic church had too much influence on politics.

9. How did DeValera get back into Irish politics?

A. In 1926 he founded the Fianna Fail party and entered Irish electoral politics. His new party was swept into power in 1932. In 1933-36, DeValera attempted to reduce British influence in the 26 counties by:

1. Withholding Land Annuities due to England. Payments totaling 5.5 million

pounds per year had been made every June and December until De Valera put an end to them in 1932. Rents were cut in half and big landlord farms were divided among the landless and small farmers. Houses were built on them for tenants.

2.   Reoccupation of ports in Cork and Donegal which had been under English control. This was the first time Irish territory was recovered with no bloodshed.

3.   Cleared the way for Irish neutrality by removing a clause from the treaty of 1921 that allowed England to occupy "road, rail and harbor facilities in time of war."

4.   Removing the oath of allegiance.

5.   Eliminating the position of governor general.

6.   Abolishing the power of the British Privy Council.

7.   Removing the references to the Crown from the constitution.

B.   Finally, in 1937 a new constitution was passed that claimed dominion over the six counties.

10. How did the Irish Free State eventually become a Republic?

In 1949, the Irish government under John Costello, cut all institutional ties with Britain and declared itself a Republic. They renounced the commonwealth, removed the British governor general and joined the United Nations. England responded with the Ireland Act of 1949 which reaffirmed the partition of Ireland.

Despite its formal independence, Ireland has remained heavily influenced by Britain and has often collaborated with Britain economically and politically on many issues.

For Further Study

Coogan, T.P. 1970. *The IRA.* Pall Mall Press, London.

Costigan, G. 1969. *The History of Modern Ireland.* Pegasus, NY. Chapters 12, 13.

Cronin, S. 1981. *Irish Nationalism.* Continuum Publishing Company, NY. Chapters 14, 15, 16, 17.

McCardle, D. 1965. *The Irish Republic.* Farrar, Straus, London.

O'Farrell, P. 1972. *Ireland's English Question.* Schocken, NY.

Strauss, E. 1961. *Irish Nationalism and British Democracy.* Columbia Univ. NY.

Part II:
British colonialism and
Irish nationalism in conflict:
1916-1995

CHAPTER ELEVEN

Origins of Partition
1916 –1921

1. What was the Easter Rising and why is it sometimes referred to as the beginning of the Irish Revolution?

In Dublin during Easter week of 1916, 1,200 rebels from the Irish Republican Brotherhood (IRB), the Irish Volunteers, and the Irish Citizen Army initiated an armed insurrection against British rule. After seven days of fierce battle between rebel and British forces, the rebellion was crushed by the numerically superior British forces. The British authorities responded to the surrender by publicly executing 16 of the leaders.

The executions shocked a complacent Irish people, rekindled a sense of nationhood and resulted in great numbers of converts to Irish republicanism.

2. Why was the British Parliamentary election of 1918 significant?

In that election 80% of the Irish people voted for candidates who supported an independent Ireland. While Britain ignored the result, the successful Irish candidates set up the first Dail Eireann (parliament) in Dublin.

The British response was to embark on a war with the Irish people. The Black and Tans and Auxiliaries were sent to Ireland to aid the Royal Irish Constabulary (RIC) in crushing the rebels.

3. What was the difference between constitutional and revolutionary Irish nationalism?

Constitutional nationalism hoped to gain independence through debate and negotiation while revolutionary nationalism advocated armed insurrection in order to gain freedom.

4. *Differentiate home rule, dominion status and independence.*

A. **Home rule** — Ireland would be granted its own parliament with power to legislate for Ireland on internal affairs while remaining under British rule.

B. **Dominion status** — independent status within the British Commonwealth including their own armed forces, revenues, law, postal services and external affairs while allowing Britain to retain naval and military bases and recognizing the ultimate sovereignty of the British crown.

C. **Independence** — complete severance of ties with Britain.

5. *How did the IRA originate?*

In January 1919 Michael Collins came to lead the Irish Republican Army (IRA) — known in Irish as *Oglaigh na h Eireann* — which was formed from the remains of the Irish Republican Brotherhood, the Irish Volunteers, and the Irish Citizen Army who fought in the Easter Rebellion of 1916. Collins directed the IRA in what became known as the Anglo-Irish War (1919-1921) to free Ireland from British rule and defend the original Dail Eireann established in 1918 (p. 102, #2).

6. *Explain something about the forerunners of the IRA?*

The historic forerunner of the IRA was the Irish Republican Brotherhood (IRB) which was founded in New York and Dublin on March 17, 1857. In the United States it was known as the Fenian Brotherhood and was founded by expatriates of the Young Ireland Movement of the 1840s (p. 54, #15). The 1848 rebellion that the Young Ireland Movement initiated was militarily unsuccessful but left a symbolic legacy of insurrection that in part inspired the ideology behind the rebellion of 1916.

The IRB or Fenian Movement attempted to free Ireland from British rule in the late 1860s.

7. What was the role of the IRA in the Anglo-Irish War (1919-21)?

It was the IRA that fought the British to a standstill in the Anglo-Irish War (p.92, #6). This was accomplished by bloody guerilla war against British forces known as the Black and Tans (p. 93, #7) and Auxiliaries. However, the revolution was aborted when a forced peace treaty kept the six northeastern counties of Ireland under British control (see #10 below).

8. What was the Government of Ireland Act of 1920?

A British Parliamentary act that officially partitioned Ireland into two sections. Ireland was to be governed by two parliaments, one in Belfast and Dublin.

This occurred without a vote of the Irish people. The *London Times* called it an immoral concept maintained by gerrymandering, police-bullying, repressive laws, British Army repression and pressure on Catholics to emigrate due to no jobs, houses or rights.

9. Why were only six out of nine counties in the province of Ulster included in the area that came to be known as Northern Ireland?

The British partition plan excluded three of Ulster's nine counties; Donegal, Monaghan and Cavan, because these counties had a large Sinn Fein (nationalist) majority: 260,000 to 70,000 unionists. Carving out these counties assured a 60 to 40% majority of unionists in the remaining six counties.

10. How did the state of Northern Ireland come into existence?

Unable to defeat the Irish militarily in the Anglo-Irish War (p. 92, #6), English Prime Minister Lloyd George was determined to thwart the movement for Irish independence. Possibly, the British felt that they could not afford to lose Ireland as they feared revolts in other parts of the Empire such as India. Lloyd George opened negotiations with representatives of the Provisional Irish government in 1921, offering home rule for the 26 counties located primarily in the south of Ireland. This entity would be known as the Irish Free State, and it was to exist under the authority of the British Crown, while the six northeast counties would remain temporarily under direct British rule. Irish Free State officials would be bound by an Oath of Allegiance to the Crown.

This offer was made under the threat of accelerating the Anglo-Irish War to a devastating level which would have included the aerial bombing of Irish cities if the offer had been rejected. The inexperienced Irish negotiators accepted and signed the treaty on December 6, 1921.

After a heated debate in the Dail Eireann, the treaty was approved by a narrow vote on January 7, 1922. A bloody civil war broke out between "republicans" who rejected the treaty and "Free Staters" who accepted it.

11. *Why did the British choose to remain in part of Ireland?*

A. For military/defensive reasons.
B. To allow the British to maintain direct and indirect control over all of Ireland.
C. To protect capitalist investment, which was concentrated in the northeast.
D. To preserve British prestige.
E. To satisfy a loyalist (p. 139, #2) majority heavily concentrated in the three counties that was a minority on the whole island.

12. *What was the Irish Civil War (1921-23) and what was its significance?*

It was a war that erupted between republican anti-treaty forces and Free State pro-treaty forces (1921-23). The Free Staters were supported and equipped by the British while the IRA split on both sides. It divided families and created many lasting emotional wounds among the Irish people.

It was a bloody confrontation in which many of Ireland's most promising political and social leaders died. The anti-treaty forces were defeated but went underground in order to carry on the fight for an undivided republic. The Irish Civil War was a period in which deep political divisions were born, and many of those divisions still resound in today's Irish political scene.

13. What would Protestants have lost in an independent Ireland?

Catholic gains in an independent Ireland would be made at the expense of Protestants who held most of the better jobs, such as the shipyards where Protestants held 90% of the jobs. The possible loss of markets due to separation from Britain could lead to a loss of jobs that were predominantly Protestant. But Protestants have integrated themselves peacefully in the 26-county republic of Ireland and share generously in the country's resources. Though Protestants only make up less than 4% of the population in the 26-counties, they hold 34% of its wealth.

14. How did gerrymandering play a role in the organization of the Northern Ireland?

The state of Northern Ireland itself was a gerrymander, excising six counties out of the original 32 counties of Ireland. In this set-up, unionists had a 60-40% majority.

At the founding of the state, nationalists were concentrated in a few larger wards where they were numerically insignificant and therefore had no clout. Unionists were dispersed over a number of smaller wards to assure they had majority control. Further, only people with taxable property could vote and in 1923 voting was also restricted to those owning land worth at least five pounds or more.

In 1921 proportional representation was abolished. In 1945 the British government exempted the six counties from universal suffrage and the abolition of business votes. This sort of manipulation resulted in situations such as in Derry whereby despite a 60% Catholic majority, Protestants held 12 Council seats while Catholics only held eight.

15. How was the economy organized in the new Northern Ireland?

Systematic job discrimination was implemented

for both state and private owned firms. Catholics got only menial jobs. Northern Ireland's Unionist Prime Minister Lord Brookeborough (1942-1963) stated the case plainly: "I recommend those people who are loyalists not to employ Catholics."

New industrial investment was centered on an area within a 30 mile radius of Belfast where 75% of the Protestants live. The area west of the River Bann which was largely nationalist (Catholic) was neglected and Derry City was deindustrialized.

More recently, when a new university was built in 1964, it was located in Coleraine rather than nationalist Derry. Even the railroad lines to Tyrone, Fermanagh and South Derry were discontinued.

In the area of housing which is largely controlled by the state, nationalists have not been provided for. For example, Dungannon which is 50% nationalist, went 24 years without a single nationalist family getting a house — in spite of the fact that 300 families were on a waiting list for at least 12 years. Even when housing was built, as in Derry and Belfast, security or voting considerations were most important.

16. How did forced emigration impact Northern Ireland?

With no jobs, houses or political rights and attacks at work and on homes, there was little hope for most nationalists. This led to selective emigration of nationalists. Between 1937-1967, 21% of the nationalist community emigrated while during the same period only 8% of the Protestants emigrated. Such a differential allowed unionists to maintain their gerrymandered majority in the six counties.

17. How did state-condoned terror play a role in the development of Northern Ireland?

Unionist politicians encouraged the Protestant working class to become sectarian by blaming Catholics for local economic problems. In the summer of 1920 Protestants started indiscriminate attacks on Catholics, burning their homes, driving them from their jobs, and committing random murders. In 1921 in Belfast, out of 93,000 Catholics, 250 were killed,11,000 were driven from their jobs and 22,000 were driven from their homes.

When Catholics fought back, the British intervened and even collaborated with UVF (Ulster Volunteer Force), a loyalist terrorist group. This included joint foot patrols. In late 1920 the British disarmed the Catholics and also formed the Royal Ulster Constabulary (RUC) a sectarian police force.

Also, in September 1920, the British cabinet approved a special constabulary, the most famous of which was the B-Specials. The B-Specials were a part-time fully armed local militia which assisted the police. Its members were primarily Protestants.

18. Characterize the government of Northern Ireland from 1920-1972?

Perhaps Unionist Prime Minister for Northern Ireland, Lord Craigavon (1921-1940), said it all: "We are a Protestant Parliament for a Protestant state."

Unionists (p. 139, #2) held complete political and military control of Northern Ireland, only exacerbating the disaffection of the nationalist/Catholic community toward the state. In effect, the government encouraged the development of a caste system of inequality, leading one Irish civil rights activist from Derry, Fionbarra O'Dochartaigh, to declare "We are the white negroes of Ireland."

Even the more "enlightened" Unionist Prime Minister for Northern Ireland, Terrence O'Neill (1963-1969), gave only patronizing consideration to the nationalist community, when he said, "If you treat Roman Catholics with due consideration and kindness, they will act like Protestants."

19. Identify the Orange Order and its significance in Northern Ireland.

It is a fraternal society dedicated to opposing Catholicism. Its members could be expelled for even attending a Catholic funeral. Almost all unionist politicians and the judiciary are orangemen. Orange halls provide meeting places for unionist political organizations. Lord Craigavon once said, "I have said I am an Orangeman first of all and a member of parliament afterwards."

Many feel that the Orange Order has been the central organ that has prevented the rise of an independent working class politic by integrating the Protestant working class into the unionist establishment. (see also p. 139, #1)

20. How was organized repression used to maintain the Orange State?

The summer of 1922 saw a massive show of military might including 30,000 A,B,C Specials; 3,000-4,000 RUC; 7,500 Territorial Army; 20,000 UVF and 16 battalions of the British Army on duty in the six counties.

The Special Powers Act of April 7, 1922 was implemented to crush the nationalists politically. This draconian Act included the following:

A. Detention without charge or trial.

B. Outlawing of organizations.

C. Imposition of a curfew and restriction of movement.

D. Prohibition of inquests.

E. Prohibition of meetings and public demonstrations.

F. Search and arrest without warrant.

G. Confiscation of property.

H. Detention of individuals up to 48 hours without an attorney.

I. Make *any* restriction they feel necessary to preserve order.

21. What is the nature of the religious division in Northern Ireland?

Religious labels are almost always substituted for political categories in Northern Ireland, causing much confusion about relations between Protestant and Catholic workers. The labels are vestiges of colonialism stemming from the early 17th century when Britain settled English and Scottish planters (who happened to be Protestant) on confiscated land in an attempt to gain greater control over the rebellious Irish province. These tenant-farming-class settlers and their descendants received privileges in the forms of land, jobs, status, and power in exchange for their support of British interests. The displaced indigenous population happened to be Catholic.

Northern Ireland was formed in 1921 at the conclusion of the Anglo-Irish war against British colonialism. Consisting of six counties that were partitioned from historic Ireland, it was designated a part of the United Kingdom. It remains under the control of former colonial elites loyal to Britain. These elites and their supporters institutionalized and maintain the system of stratification characterized by the unequal distribution of resources and power.

Those loyal to Britain, known as unionists or loyalists, were and are mostly Protestant in their faith. They were given political, economic, and social privileges. However, Protestant privilege is delineated along class lines. The privileged elites dominate finance, housing, industry, the police, the judiciary, civil services, and all public services. In short, they control the state, In actuality, members of the Protestant working class receive little in return for their loyalty. Greater access to housing and jobs than that afforded their Catholic counterparts can be counted among their benefits.

Members of the Protestant working class are often referred to as loyalists. The term frequently connotes militant unionism. Although most Protestants desire continued unity with Britain, all are not extremists nor members of loyalist paramilitary organizations. However, the extreme forces of loyalist ideology permeate life in Northern Ireland. As Protestant unemployment has sharply increased over the past several years, working-class people have become more fearful and defensive. Many Protestant people are living in ghetto housing and struggling with very low wages for survival.

Those opposed to union with Britain, known as nationalists, were and are mostly Catholic in their religious faith. They have been systematically denied the most basic human rights.

The British have used religion to divert attention from the real reasons for the struggle: economic and political deprivation.

CHAPTER TWELVE

From civil rights to civil war (1968-1972)

1. How did the Northern Ireland civil rights movement develop?

It began in the late 1960s as a non-sectarian, non-violent movement modelled on the work of Dr. Martin Luther King, Jr. in the United States. It protested gerrymandering and discrimination in housing, jobs, and services. One of its themes was "one man, one vote" because voting rights were based on property ownership, which shut-out the economically disadvantged nationalist community. Public meetings, demonstrations and protest marches were held.

The official Northern Ireland Civil Rights Association (NICRA) began in 1968 when the Wolfe Tone Society and Campaign for Social Justice combined along the lines of the National Council of Civil Liberties in Britain.

2. Identify the Northern Ireland Civil Rights Association and its significance.

The Northern Ireland Civil Rights Association (NICRA) was founded in 1967 by the Campaign for Social Justice, some Irish republicans and other groups. It was supposed to be a multi-party lobbying organization that would draw attention to discrimination in housing and employment. It played an important role in the civil rights protest marches in the 1960s. Since the 1970s, it has been dominated by the "Stickies," formally known as the Workers Party, and Communist Party members of Ireland. It is largely irrelevant today.

3. What was the nature of the state in Northern Ireland at the start of the civil rights movement?

A. Nationalists were on the bottom rungs of the

social, economic and political ladder. Jobs were scarce for Catholics/nationalists, and because voting rights were based on property ownership, a lop-sided equation of poverty and political powerlessness existed for the nationalist community, compared to jobs and political power for loyalists.

B. Periodic pogroms were used to drive nationalists out of neighborhoods and the workplace, e.g. in 1969, loyalist pograms in the nationalist areas of Belfast resulted in 524 nationalist homes being burned down, according to reports in the *Irish News*. Again in 1971, two whole streets were burned out and 200 houses destroyed.

C. The police, known as the Royal Ulster Constabulary (RUC), and their auxiliaries (B-Specials) constantly harassed and intimidated the nationalist population.

4. What were the major problems for the civil rights movement?

The equality it asked for went against the basic values upon which Northern Ireland was founded: inequality, privilege and sectarianism. There was really little or no political center in the six counties. Most Protestants felt reforms were unacceptable, while most Catholics viewed them as too mild.

The British on the other hand did not want Northern Ireland to collapse. So they did not antagonize or try to control unionist excesses. This in turn led to Catholic distrust and unionist sectarian provocation.

5. What was the loyalist response to the civil rights movement?

A swift and brutal backlash—characterized by beatings, stonings, and killing of civil rights marchers took place. A civil rights march from Derry to Belfast in January, 1969 was ambushed and brutally attacked at Burntollet Bridge by a loyalist mob as RUC (Royal Ulster Constabulary) looked on and some even joined in the attack.

Nationalist areas were attacked and burned by loyalist mobs (see # 3. B.), often supported by RUC and their auxiliaries, the B-Specials. Many people were left homeless and others migrated to the border areas of the 26 counties.

6. How did the British government react to the questions raised by the civil rights movement?

The demands were largely ignored, whitewashed, or referred to tribunals and commissions. The B-specials were disbanded but reconstituted as the Ulster Defence Regiment (UDR) under the control of the British Army instead of RUC. Over 50% of the initial recruits were ex-B-specials and almost all were Protestants.

Some gerrymandering and property qualifications for voting were changed. Lip service was paid to fair employment and housing, but local loyalists remained in political control, and military control considerations became paramount in planning housing structure and housing location. Job discrimination against nationalists has continued.

7. How did Britain respond to loyalist violence?

The British Army was sent to Northern Ireland in 1969 under the guise of being a peacekeeping force to separate the warring factions, but the real purpose was to prop up a crumbling loyalist state. The army quickly took the loyalist side and became a focal point for the increased repression of the nationalist population.

8. What was Bloody Sunday and what was its significance for the future of the non-violent civil rights movement?

On January 30, 1972, British paratroopers shot and killed 14 unarmed civil rights demonstrators on the streets of Derry. A British commission under Lord Widgery whitewashed the action and the commanding officer of the unit was later decorated with the Order of the British Empire by the Queen. It was obvious from this point on that the government could not be reformed by peaceful non-violent means. The event and its aftermath hardened the nationalist community and encouraged recruiting for revolutionary groups.

9. Identify the Nationalist Party and its significance.

The Nationalist Party was founded in 1921 as an anti-partition party although it was not known officially by this name until the mid-1950s. It was a middle class Catholic, clergy-dominated party that often cooperated with the unionist government. The civil rights movement swept the nationalists aside, and in the elections of 1969 and 1973, the Party lost all their seats in Stormont. The Party is now defunct with their membership largely absorbed by the SDLP.

10. What was the status of the IRA at the start of the civil rights movement and how did this affect the ability of the IRA to fulfill its traditional role?

Under the leadership of Cathal Goulding, the IRA had drifted toward an ultra-left orientation that gave up the armed struggle. Some of their arms were actually sold to Welsh nationalists. The unarmed IRA was thus poorly equipped to defend the nationalist communities against the loyalist backlash to the civil rights movement. But vigilante groups emerged as defense committees to protect neighborhoods from loyalist pograms. These "vigilante" groups formed the grassroots basis for the resurgence of the IRA.

CHAPTER THIRTEEN

Republicans and a war of liberation

1. Identify the Border War of the 1950s and its historic significance.

In 1956-62, numerous destructive attacks were mounted by the IRA against customs posts and Royal Ulster Constabulary barracks. The campaign had substantial support in the border counties on both sides of the partition line. It served to keep the tradition of armed resistance alive and produced folk heroes such as Sean South and Feargal O'Hanlon, who waged rural guerilla warfare against the British forces in border counties.

2. What caused the split in the IRA during 1969-1970?

The Provisional IRA (PIRA) was formed in 1969-1970 following an ideological split in the movement. The IRA, since 1963 under the leadership of Cathal Goulding had drifted toward an ultra-left orientation that excluded the guerilla warfare that had been its hallmark. In 1969 when loyalist attacks on nationalist areas occurred, the organization was not in position to fill its traditional role as a defense force in nationalist areas.

When the so-called "official" wing of the IRA suggested recognizing both the Stormont (Northern Ireland) and Dublin Parliaments, the more staunchly nationalist members separated and formed the Provisional IRA in January, 1970. Though a minority at the time of the split, the Provisionals began to grow. In June of 1970 the Belfast Brigade of the PIRA successfully resisted a loyalist invasion and pogrom in the Short Strand, an isolated nationalist area in east Belfast.

The Provisionals espoused a traditional Irish republicanism congruent with the Proclamation of 1916 and were prepared to use arms to defend the nationalist areas. British Army oppression in northeast Ireland aided the growth and development of the PIRA. The "officials" or "stickies" eventually gave up military action and have gradually moved toward a collaborationist position that recognizes the British presence in Ireland as necessary. Known today as the Workers Party, their membership and influence in the north has dwindled to an insignificant number. In the 26 counties, a split from the Workers Party known as the Democratic Left was formed in the early 1990s.

3. Why is it said that the Provisional IRA (PIRA) arose from the ashes of the civil rights movement?

The violent destruction of the civil rights movement in the backlash of loyalist bigotry and the British government's complicity renewed demands for a nationalist defense force. The dormant IRA rose from the ashes of the confrontation between the civil rights movement and loyalist reactionaries to defend the nationalist people against further pogroms.

4. Characterize the modern phase of IRA activity in Ireland.

The IRA has become the inheritor of the tradition seeking national self-determination and liberation from British rule. The nationalist population recognizes them as a positive force, even in the face of British-manufactured propaganda which attempts to portray them as terrorists. The IRA's main objectives are to force the British out of the six counties and ensure national self-determination for the Irish people. They have waged a long war of attrition that has been offensive as well as defensive. Strategy has ranged from strategic bombing of economic and government targets, to sophisticated electronically controlled attacks against occupation forces. Great care is taken to avoid civilian casualties, with a great number of operations aborted to prevent civilian casualties. This is necessary to maintain support and credibility. Even damaging errors are admitted in an effort to maintain the movement's credibility.

The economic losses, casualties, and constant harassment by republican forces have all been geared toward forcing the British to seek a political solution and withdraw. Even the British military's own Glover Report (p. 120, #9) admits they cannot defeat the IRA.

5. What was internment without trial and its long-term significance?

On August 9, 1971, at 4:00 a.m. British forces staged a series of dawn raids on nationalist areas of Belfast, seized 342 people and interned them without trial or charge in special concentration camps. Over the next four years a total of 2,158 interment orders were issued. Internees were badly treated and some were subjected to systematic deprivation and torture.

It destroyed what remained of any illusions about British democracy, even for moderate nationalists. It also generated levels of support and solidarity unknown before. The republican movement grew rather than died.

As author J. Bowyer Bell noted: "Internment did not crush the Provos but unleashed them."

6. Identify the following republican groups.

Provisional Sinn Fein was founded in 1969-1970 as a result of a split in the Sinn Fein party. Provisional Sinn Fein, with offices originally in Kevin Street, Dublin, took a strong social populist stance and a militant approach to partition. It is the most committed voice for republican ideology today. Sinn Fein popular support has been underscored by recent electoral successes at the Council level elections in northeast Ireland. In local council elections in Spring, 1993, Sinn Fein candidates in Belfast won more first preference votes than any other party. Now known simply as Sinn Fein.

Contrary to media depictions, Sinn Fein and the IRA are not one monolithic organization. Sinn Fein is a distinctly separate organization that focuses on political action and mobilization. While Sinn Fein and the IRA are separate groups, they are working toward the same ultimate goal of a reunited Ireland.

Provisional IRA (Provos) was founded in 1970 to defend the nationalist ghettos against loyalist attack. It is the main guerilla force in Ireland and a lineal descendant of the "old" IRA dating back to the Anglo-Irish war of 1919-22.

The Provos enjoy broad based nationalist support and have fought an effective 25 year war against 30,000 British forces in the province. It is a formidable force that even the British Army admits cannot be defeated. The leadership is young, dedicated and prepared to wage a long guerilla war of attrition.

Irish Republican Socialist Party (IRSP) was founded in 1974 by Bernadette Devlin McAliskey and Seamus Costello in order to combine Marxist ideology with a strong nationalist focus. Its founders were largely disenchanted Official Sinn Fein (Stickies) supporters. They wanted a more militant approach on the question of partition. They are not anti-Provisional IRA. One of their major leaders Miriam Daly, an economics professor, was assassinated during the H-Block protests in 1980 by either loyalists or the SAS. Party membership has dwindled in recent years, with many choosing to join Sinn Fein.

Irish National Liberation Army (INLA) was founded in 1975 as the armed wing of the IRSP, made up largely of ex-Official IRA who wanted to continue a military struggle. Both the IRSP and INLA contended that national liberation and socialist revolution should be pursued simultaneously. They are a small, hard-core guerilla army that in the past cooperated with the Provos in the struggle against Britain. It was the INLA that assassinated Airey Neave, the anti-Irish, racist conservative party spokesperson on British occupied Ireland. Today the group has been ripped apart by internal fighting and assassinations. Republicans have called for their disbandment.

Peoples Democracy (PD) was founded in October, 1968, in Belfast, as a leftist student civil rights group. It played an important part in the civil rights movement, especially the protest marches of January, 1969.

It has been active in the south and north of Ireland. It was the only left-wing group to directly support the Provos. It has been plagued by factional rifts that have limited its effectiveness.

The Irish Independence Party was founded in October of 1977 by Frank McManus and Fergus McAteer. It united independent nationalists with former members of the moribund Nationalist Party (p. 114, #9). The party identified the British presence as the root cause of violence and demanded troop withdrawal. Party member John Turnly, a prominent Protestant and former British Army officer, was assassinated in 1980 by loyalists due to his support of the republican prisoners demands for prisoner of war status.

7. How did the IRA reorganize in the 1970s?

In late 1976, in response to penetration by informers and spies, the IRA reorganized. The Republican Army moved from its traditional brigade/battalion/company structure to one built on a cell system. This structure consists of three- or four-person active service units (ASU) specializing in such missions as intelligence gathering, sniping, bombing and punishment. It was hoped that this system would limit knowledge of volunteer identity and whereabouts to the smallest number of IRA personnel.

Internal discipline was strengthened after 1977 with the executions of spies. At the same time volunteers began to receive more intensive political education in order to more fully understand every phase of the struggle and to more effectively resist interrogation. The women's group, Cumann na mBan, was disbanded with women fully integrated into the IRA. This move affirmed a long tradition of militant female republicans, symbolized effectively by Countess Markievicz, an active participant in the Easter rebellion of 1916. The new structure has proven neither perfect nor complete in its implementation but it has, especially in urban areas, allowed the IRA to survive increasingly sophisticated British pressure and to fight on more effectively.

8.   *Identify some of the major strategies used by the modern day IRA.*

The strategies have ranged from the selective bombing of economic and government targets, to sophisticated electronically controlled attacks against crown forces. Great care is taken to avoid civilian casualties, with even the British Army attesting to the reliability of IRA warnings. Planned IRA operations are often aborted if the risk to civilians in the area is judged to be too great. Civilians are constantly warned by the IRA to steer clear of possible military targets. Even damaging errors are admitted in an effort to maintain credibility.

The economic losses, casualties and constant harassment by Republican forces have all been geared toward forcing the British to seek a political solution and withdraw. Even the British military admit they cannot defeat the IRA— but the IRA can destroy the will of the British to stay.

9.   *What was the Glover Report and its significance?*

It was an internal British Army document made public in 1978 that admitted that the British Army could not defeat the IRA. It also maintained that the IRA had no direct international connections or Marxist orientation. The report viewed the IRA as a well-trained, highly-disciplined guerilla force that was a nationalist movement with working class roots.

10. *Does the IRA have much support in Ireland?*

No guerilla army can survive without support of the people in the community. The growth and development of the IRA in the face of massive sophisticated repression by the British is evidence of support. IRA hunger strikers were elected to parliament in both the six counties and the 26-county republic of Ireland. Polls throughout Ireland indicate significant support for IRA goals as well as methods.

11. *Describe the IRA's relationship to other revolutionary movements.*

The IRA has strong ideological affinities for third world liberation struggles such as SWAPO, the ANC, the PLO and Polisario as well as those of the Basques (ETA) Corsicans and Bretons. The historical parallels with the 800 year struggle in Ireland against British colonization are readily understood. They do not however admit to having anything in common with the Red Brigades of Italy and the Red Army Faction in Germany.

12. *What is the IRA's position with respect to loyalist paramilitaries?*

The IRA has generally made it a matter of policy not to attack the Ulster Defence Association (UDA) or Ulster Volunteer Force (UVF) except in self defense since their fight is with British occupation forces. However, occasionally the IRA executes loyalist paramilitaries who are held responsible for the sectarian murder of nationalists.

13. *What is the significance of:*

An Cumann Cabhrach— a Dublin-based organization that aids the dependents of republican prisoners.

Green Cross—a part of An Cumann Cabrach that operates in Belfast to aid prisoners' dependents.

Irish Northern Aid Committee— an American organization founded in 1970 by Michael Flannery, Jack McGowan and Jack McCarthy that raises funds in the United States for the families of Irish political prisoners. It also promotes public education on the situation in northeast Ireland. Better known as Noraid, it has been subject to much government scrutiny and harassment in the United States.

14. *Differentiate nationalists and republicans.*

Nationalists—those people who want to see Ireland united into one nation.

Republicans—more militant nationalists who are willing to use physical force to drive Britain from the six counties and allow the people of all Ireland to decide its political future.

15. What has been the role of Irish Americans in the struggle?

The Irish American organizations Irish Northern Aid Committee (NORAID) and Clan na Gael are actively involved in fund raising for prisoners families and raising U.S. awareness about Ireland's struggle. Other groups such as the Irish American Unity Conference (IAUC), and the American Irish Political Education Committee focus activity around political lobbying and public education and awareness programs.

Irish American activists must maintain and defend their beliefs in the face of much criticism, poor press and direct harassment by the government. Irish American sentimentalists do exist, but they are not a significant element among political activists.

16. What is the significance of the names used to describe the areas of Ireland that are under British rule and those that are not?

Northern Ireland — the British name for the part of Ireland that is under the jurisdiction of the United Kingdom.

northeast Ireland — a term often used as an alternative to Northern Ireland. It implies non-recognition of the political legitimacy of the state of Northern Ireland.

six counties and **26-counties** — In its entirety, Ireland consists of 32 counties, the northeast six of which were claimed by the British as Northern Ireland. In an effort to emphasize that Ireland is one whole nation, many nationalists refer to the **six counties** when speaking of those areas under British rule, and the **26-counties** when speaking of the southern portion of the state that is not under direct British rule.

Ulster—a term used by unionists to refer to the six counties. Use of this term is actually inaccurate because the province of Ulster consists of nine, not six counties. The excluded counties of Ulster were purposely cut out to assure a loyalist majority for the state of Northern Ireland.

British-occupied Ireland — a termed used by some activists opposing British rule in Ireland, especially those in the United States, in order to emphasize the nature of the British position in the six counties.

The north — a term that attempts to be neutral, but one should keep in mind that the northern most part of the province of Ulster is county Donegal, which is part of the 26-counties.

The Orange State — a reference to the government of Northern Ireland as an entity that has maintained and protected the interests of the loyalists (p.139, #2) and repressed the nationalists (p. 121, #14).

CHAPTER FOURTEEN

The British response

1. *What has been the role of the British Army in the current phase of "The Troubles"?*

A. The British Army was initially brought in to prop up the crumbling loyalist state of Northern Ireland in 1969, not to protect the nationalist community from loyalist violence.

B. The Army's role today is to fight the IRA as well as harass and intimidate the nationalist population.

C. The Army also serves to back up the local occupation forces, the RUC and UDR, in case they falter.

D. Evidence indicates that the Army has acted in collusion with loyalist death squads in planning and executing murders of nationalist community members.

E. Even during the current (1994-95) ceasefire by the IRA and loyalist paramilitary groups, British Army presence is still heavy, especially in the border areas. The Peace Action Monitor group reported more than 3,000 incidents of crown forces' patrols in one month alone, indicating a continued high level of militarization, harassment and intimidation.

2. *What was the Falls Road Curfew and its significance for army-community relations?*

On July 3, 1970 the British enforced a three day curfew on the lower Falls Road area, cutting it off from the rest of Belfast. During this time hundreds of homes were wrecked, mass arrests carried out and three people shot dead. The curfew was broken when thousands of people lead by the women marched into the lower Falls tearing down the barriers and pushing the soldiers aside.

3. *Identify the Northern Ireland Emergency Provisions Act of 1973.*

It was called the Emergency Powers Act passed in 1973. This new act was simply a refinement of the Special Powers Act (p. 109, #20). It established the "conveyer belt" justice system, which includes detention without cause, brutal interrogation, forced confessions, and non-jury Diplock Courts.

4. *What is the Kitson strategy?*

A strategy practiced in the six counties from about 1975 on and devised by Brigadier General Kitson, a British counterinsurgency specialist.

It includes some of the following practices:

A. Passing emergency regulations to aid the military campaign.

B. Formulation of an integrated nationwide intelligence organization consisting of units known as MRF and MI-5.

C. Joint military and civilian control at all levels (planning, policy making and administration).

D. Strengthening the local police (RUC) and armed forces (UDR) so that their loyalty is beyond question.

E. Attempt to isolate the insurgents from popular support through:
1. Some concessions.
2. Harassment.
3. Threat of harassment.
4. "Dirty tricks."

5. *What is a Diplock Court and how does it operate?*

The Diplock Courts were created in 1973 by Lord Diplock. They are special non-jury courts for those suspected of "terrorist activities."

A. One judge alone makes the decision. They have a 95% conviction rate.

B. Independent witnesses are rarely present.

C. Often the charge is not even discussed; the political context of maintaining British control and authority are often highlighted as the

125

most important principles to protect.

D. Most of the evidence would be inadmissable in a London court.

E. In 90% of cases heard by these Courts, the chief evidence involves signed statements by the accused, often obtained by physical or mental abuse.

F. Onus is on the defendant to substantiate allegations of torture, etc.

G. Security forces cannot be cross-examined.

H. Prisoners can spend an indefinite time in jail awaiting trial (known as remand).

6. What is the Prevention of Terrorism Act?

An act passed in Britain in 1974 and amended in 1976 (it was extended to the six counties in 1976). It gives the state the following powers:

A. Power to proscribe or ban any organization appearing to the Northern Ireland Home Secretary to be involved in "terrorism." It was broadened in 1976 to cover individuals who raise support for terrorism, e.g., collect money, sell literature.

B. Power to exclude from Britain anyone the Home Secretary believes to be involved in "terror."

C. Power to detain (or arrest) without warrant for up to 7 days without charge.

D. In 1976, it was made an offense to not pass on anti-terrorist information to the authorities.

E. Police have the right to stop and search anyone they suspect of terrorism.

7. What was the criminalization policy of the British and the republican response?

On March 1, 1976, the government withdrew special category status which separated "political prisoners" from common criminals. It was an attempt to de-politicize the conflict and eliminate the concept of a national liberation movement. On September 14, 1976, when Irish political prisoner Kieran Nugent refused to wear a prison uniform, he was immediately thrown into a cell with only a blanket. He was subsequently joined by others and the blanket protest was underway.

The blanket men were confined to their cells without clothes, reading material, and furniture except for a mattress which was taken away during the day. Chamber pots used by the prisoners were continually kicked onto the floor by prison guards, and thus was born the dirty protest, in which prisoners smeared the over-flowing excrement on the cell walls in order to keep the floors dry.

8. Why did the hunger strikes of 1980-81 begin?

After four years of living under increasingly intolerable conditions created by the blanket and dirty protests, the prisoners launched a hunger strike in the fall of 1980. They hoped to force concessions of special category status. They felt they were captured in a war of liberation and, thus should be accorded prisoner of war status.

In December 1980, with one prisoner, Sean McKenna, near death and Christmas approaching, the British government seemingly acceded to the prisoners' demands. The prisoners were presented with a document of the government's concessions and the strike was ended. It seems now that the Thatcher government wanted to avert a death during the Christmas season when world pressure and indignation might be at its height. However, in January the government reneged on the concessions and resumed criminalization. Even Irish Catholic Cardinal O'Fiaich said that the British had gone back on their word. A new hunger strike began on March 1, 1981, led by Bobby Sands, an IRA volunteer. This strike focussed world attention on the situation in Ireland but resulted in the death of ten young Irishmen between May and August of 1981.

9. What were the hunger strikers' five demands?

A. The right not to wear prison uniforms.

B. The right not to do prisoner's prison work.

C. The right to associate freely with other political prisoners.

D. Restoration of the right to earn remission (early release time).

E. The right to a weekly visit, letter, parcel, and the right to organize their own educational and recreational pursuits.

10. Did the IRA play a direct role in the initiation of the hunger strikes of 1980-81?

The IRA did not control the hunger strikes and actually opposed the use of this strategy. The hunger strikes were initiated by the prisoners themselves in an attempt to alter the criminalization policy (p. 126, #7) of the British government. The hunger strike was a weapon of last resort. The IRA fully supported the hunger strikers once the action was initiated. It is also well to remember that three of the dead hunger strikers were INLA (p. 118, #6) members, an organization that was not under control of the IRA.

11. How did the hunger strikes end?

Under mounting pressure on the prisoners' families by the church and Margaret Thatcher's obvious contempt for world opinion, some of the prisoners' families gave permission to administer food to the hunger strikers after they lapsed into unconsciousness in October 1981.

12. What were the effects of the hunger strikes?

British injustice in Ireland was exposed massively before the whole world. The election of Bobby Sands to the British Parliament while on hunger strike disproved the British contention that the revolutionaries had little support. Later on, the election of hunger strikers Kieran Doherty to the Irish Dail (Parliament) disproved a similar contention for the south of Ireland.

The ultimate effects of the hunger strike period will be determined by history. Some effects are already apparent. The resolve of nationalists to rid the country of British rule has been strengthened in yet another generation. For them, there is no turning back. Grassroots organization and political participation has become a significant part of the struggle, as witnessed by the success of Sinn Fein in electoral politics throughout the 1980s and 90s. Also, the worldwide support network for the republican movement has been strengthened and extended.

13. Identify the international agencies that documented the use of torture and inhumane treatment against Irish nationalist prisoners and what was the nature of their charges?

Amnesty International, 1972 — reported systematic torture by the British in northeast Ireland.

European Commission on Human Rights, 1978 — found the British government guilty of torture of Irish prisoners.

European Court of Human Rights, 1978 — found the British government guilty of inhumane and degrading treatment of Irish prisoners.

Amnesty International, 1978 — reaffirmed and presents new evidence of use of systematic torture by authorities in northeast Ireland.

Bennett Report, 1978 — a British government report documenting mistreatment of Irish political prisoners.

Amnesty International, 1988 — documents concerns about killings in disputed circumstances and the use of paid perjurers to convict.

Amnesty International, 1991 — documents new cases of ill-treatment of prisoners, violation of rights to fair trial, collusion between security forces and armed groups and killings in disputed circumstances.

Amnesty International, 1994 — details the chief aspects of Army collusion with loyalist armed groups in the planning and execution of political killings.

14. What is meant by Ulsterization and what is its significance?

It refers to attempts beginning in the mid- to late 1970s to turn over most of the visible military functions to local forces such as the RUC and UDR with the British Army remaining for backup. It is an attempt to make the situation look like a local disturbance rather than a war of liberation. It also enhances the possibility of a loyalist backlash since most of the UDR and RUC that come under attack are loyalist. This further polarizes the loyalist and nationalist working classes. It further reinforces the British propaganda that the conflict is a religious conflict.

15. What evidence exists for the use of "dirty tricks" by the British to discredit the nationalists?

The London Times, unionist writer Kennedy Lindsay, and others have documented the use of bank robberies, assassinations, bombings, kidnappings, and other techniques in an effort to discredit republican forces. The object was to produce alienation in the community and among sympathetic outsiders with respect to the legitimacy of the republican cause.

In 1972 the Littlejohn Brothers, in the employ of British intelligence, bombed Liberty Hall in Dublin, making it appear to be an IRA job. The public furor that followed allowed the Irish government to pass an amendment to the Offenses Against the State Act which was aimed at further repressing the IRA. In 1974 bombs were planted in Dublin and Monaghan by loyalists who were aided by the SAS (p. 131, #16.D). The bombs were planted in busy rush hour locations and killed five people in Monaghan, 26 in Dublin. Again, an effort was taken to make the IRA appear responsible.

16. Identify the following occupation forces:

A. **Royal Ulster Constabulary** (RUC) was founded as a northern police force in 1922. In reality, it is a heavily armed paramilitary force rather than a civil police force. It has always been strongly Protestant, loyalist and anti-Catholic.

It has largely served to defend the Orange State. In spite of documented violations of prisoner rights and harassment of the Catholic minority, Britain is rapidly making it the primary security force in British occupied Ireland.

B. **B-Specials** were an auxiliary paramilitary force organized in 1920 by the British. They were part-time armed aids under the control

of the RUC. They were predominantly Protestant and often used brutality against nationalists. They were disbanded in 1969 after
openly aggressive behavior against civil rights
protesters. Many B-Specials then joined the
UDR which was organized to replace it.

C. **Ulster Defence Regiment** (UDR) is a locally
recruited militia attached to the British Army.
It was founded in April, 1970, to replace the
infamous B-Specials; it was supposed to be
non-sectarian and lightly armed, but it is 98%
Protestant and has become a heavily armed
appendage of the British Army. Members of
the UDR have been involved in many sectarian killings and often have proven connections with the UDA and UFF. They are referred to in the press as "part-time" soldiers.

D. **Special Air Services** (SAS) is a secret elite unit
of the British Army. They have conducted
terror and assassination campaigns in both
the north and south of Ireland. It's a no-holds-
barred operation that engages in murder,
frame-ups, bombings, and kidnapping. Its
counter-revolutionary operations have often
resulted in civilian deaths that were blamed
on the IRA, or less often, on the UDA. It has
been active in the North since at least 1975,
especially in the border areas.

E. **Military Reaction Force** (MRF) are armed
plain-clothes squads that patrol in unmarked
cars or under the guise of ordinary business.
They have been accused of some sectarian
killings, and possibly are SAS connected.

F. **Royal Irish Regiment**— On July 1, 1992 the
UDR was combined with the Royal Irish Rangers, a regular unit in the British Army to form
the Royal Irish Regiment with 6,650 members. It will consist largely of ex-UDR soldiers
since the Royal Irish Rangers had only 1,195
soldiers and this number has been cut in half.

**17. *Characterize the logistical nature of SAS
activity in Ireland.***

Small parties of SAS carry out the following
tasks:

A. Collection of information on and the movement of insurgent forces (IRA).
B. The ambush and murder of insurgents.
C. Assassination and demolition of targets in insurgent areas.
D. Border surveillance, which they cross at will.

18. What is the "Shoot to Kill" policy?

A policy prevalent throughout the 1980s whereby the military and police in British-occupied Ireland were granted immunity from prosecution in cases where unarmed "suspects" are killed under suspicious circumstances. The Stalker inquiry in 1984 investigated RUC involvement in this shoot to kill policy, but was aborted when it appeared that Police Chief John Stalker was about to confirm RUC participation in shoot to kill tactics. Another investigation was commissioned but that report too was suppressed under the claim of "national security."

19. What are supergrasses and what is their significance?

A. Selected prisoners are offered money, a new identify and life in another country, protection for their families and freedom from prosecution in exchange for providing "Queen's" evidence to implicate nationalists on so-called "terrorist" charges. This tactic was most heavily used throughout the 1980s.
B. The prisoners chosen are often second offenders facing long prison terms.
C. The informers are totally isolated while awaiting the trial so family and community pressure will not lead them to recant.
D. The Bill of Indictment has removed the necessity for a preliminary hearing thus:
   1. Eliminating a confrontation with the accused defendant as well as distressed family members
   2. Preventing the defense counsel from evaluating and probing the evidence against the defendant
E. The informer thus does not have to be pro-

duced until evidence is given at the trial itself.

F. Informers that have backed down indicate that the police coach and direct them as to what they should testify to and who they wanted implicated.

20. What is strip searching?

Since 1982 female republican prisoners have been strip searched intensively and regularly in both England and the six counties. One woman reported being strip searched twice a day for six months while undergoing trial in Belfast. It is not a security measure but an attempt to harass, intimidate and degrade prisoners.

Between November 1982 and September 1987 4,000 strip searches were carried out and nothing of a security nature was discovered.

The women are stripped and all body openings are examined, even the soles of the feet must be lifted for observation and sanitary napkins removed for inspection.

Insulting and dehumanizing comments about the prisoners body are made by the inspecting or observing officers. The searches are often carried out in a violent manner. Since most of the prison officers are loyalists this exacerbates the resentments and tensions of strip searching.

The stress on the prisoners is great, characterized by vomiting, cessation of menstruation, and weight loss.

Even a prisoner's baby under the age of one was subjected to strip search. One woman strip-searched after the birth of her daughter was forced to remove sanitary protection and breast pads.

Strip-searching is also an attempt to intimidate and pressure the families of prisoners, since the knowledge of this degrading treatment can be very disturbing to them.

21. How has Britain managed the news on the war in Ireland?

Techniques range from outright censorship in the form of a broadcast ban which forbids interviews with members of proscribed organizations, to self-censorship, to selective reporting of all or part of a story including:

A. Lying.
B. Misuse of religious labels.
C. Use of emotive terminology.
D. Use of anti-Irish racism.
E. Ignoring government violence or torture.
F. Censorship of news shows and documentary films.
G. Threats of prosecution against news people.

British media analyst, Liz Curtis, documents the case against the news in her book *Ireland, the Propaganda War*.

22. *What is the plastic bullet controversy in Ireland?*

Britain defies a European Parliament ban and continues to arm its occupation forces with plastic bullets as crowd control weapons in northeast Ireland. The bullets, which are four inches long and one and a half inches in diameter and fired at 160-200 miles per hour, have resulted in the death of 17 people, including seven children under the age of 15, as well as scores of serious injuries. They are used to intimidate and drive political protest from the streets.

CHAPTER FIFTEEN

Technology of social control

1. How has physical fragmentation of nationalist areas played a role in control by the government?

Between 1969 and 1973, 60,000 people were forced to leave their homes in the six counties. This was the largest population move in Europe since World War II. Relocation by the government was aimed at destruction of militant nationalist ghettoes and breaking down family and community support networks. The elderly were often isolated from the young in order to prevent cultural transmission. New estates, like Twinbrook, were also constructed far out, away from other nationalist areas.

In August 1972, during Operation Motorman, the British Army invaded the nationalist areas and established a string of forts such as Ft. Jericho in Belfast. Police and army barracks overlook all nationalist areas. In the mid-1970s the construction of a ring road (the M-1 Carriage Way) in Belfast provided security forces with easy access to nationalist areas.

2. What is the nature of surveillance techniques in the nationalist communities?

Community surveillance is massive and diverse. British forces use the most sophisticated surveillance apparatus available anywhere. Cameras mounted above housing estates monitor entry and exit from a neighborhood. They are equipped with zoom lenses and night sight devices and are used for both identification and general snooping. Listening devices are mounted on posts, buildings, and planted in houses. Phones are tapped, including private homes, clubs and public telephones.

House searches without warrant are conducted

to gather information about houses and occupants. This information is logged into massive data banks maintained on computers. House searches are usually carried out at dawn (4:30 a.m.) and are very destructive. Panelling and floor boards are routinely ripped out; cement floors are destroyed with jack hammers. Helicopters are stationed over all nationalist areas. They are capable of selecting one person out of an area and transmitting his or her picture to headquarters where it is matched up with data that reveals detailed personal information. Infrared cameras can detect vegetation and earth movement.

A computer system at Lisburn military complex contains complex data on nationalists such as:

A. Personal information: age, address, physical description, special characteristics, daily routine, places frequented.

B. Census information about a given dwelling: residents' names, pet names and physical characteristics such as color of doors, wallpaper, placement of furniture, security devices, etc.

Road checks and street harassment are common. Check points are everywhere and periodic arrests, detainment, threats and physical abuse are common. Road and street checks are equipped with computer systems. Listening devices are also placed in the approaches to road blocks to monitor comments made by passersby that may be used to justify a search.

In addition to the data collected by police and military, all information collected through social and health services is added to the military data banks. Intelligence gathering is **not** directed at known suspected activists, but at the entire nationalist population. The government, it seems, considers most nationalists as potential "terrorists."

3. To what extent is personal surveillance used by British forces?

Every nationalist over 14 years of age has a computerized record. Harassment of individuals on the street or at home is common. It includes street searches, house searches, helicopter surveillance, the use of spy cameras and listening devices, and periodic arrests and interrogation for up to seven days.

4. What is the nature of military and police interrogation abuses in the six counties?

The abuse of prisoners has been confirmed by Amnesty International five times (1972, 1978, 1988, 1991, 1994), European Court of Human Rights (1978), European Commission on Human Rights (1978). Dr. Robert Irwin and other doctors reported physical abuse of prisoners and resigned from their jobs in 1979. Britain is the worst offender in Europe of the Charter of Human Rights, including 21 censures.

Sensory deprivation techniques and physical abuse are common during interrogation at centers such as Castlereagh in Belfast. Five techniques of abuse have been identified in the six counties, including:

A. **Hooding:** with dark colored cloth bag, except during interrogation.

B. **Noise:** held in a room with continued high-pitch noise except during interrogation.

C. **Enforced posture:** facing walls with hands high overhead, legs spread, 2 or 3 days, whil batons were used to maintain posture.

D. **Sleep deprivation:** not allowed to sleep for 2 or 3 days.

E. **Food deprivation:** no food for 2 or 3 days or given dry bread and dirty water.

In 1971, a group of prisoners were hooded and threatened with being dropped from a helicopter.

5. How is the legal system used as a tool of military control?

The legal system is used to complement military repression of nationalist communities. It has become a tool of intimidation, harassment and imprisonment for nationalists.

The legal apparatus includes:

A. **Emergency Provisions Act of 1973** (p. 124, #3)

which replaced and extended the Special Powers Act of 1922.

B. **The Prevention of Terrorism Act of 1976** allows arrest without charge and detention for seven days.

C. **The Criminal Justice Act of 1970** can result in six months in jail for "riotous" behavior.

D. **The Flags and Emblems Act of 1954** can lead to the arrest of anyone displaying a flag or emblem that the government deems dangerous. This most usually means displaying the Irish tri-color flag.

E. **Non-jury Diplock Courts** started in 1973 dole out justice with a single judge acting as both judge and jury. These courts have a 95% conviction rate, and 80% of the convictions are based on self-incriminating evidence obtained under duress. Much of the evidence would be inadmissable in a regular court and the occupation forces can't be cross-examined in court. These courts include indefinite remand (time in jail while waiting to be charged and have a trial) and on occasion the use of paid perjurers to convict.

CHAPTER SIXTEEN

The loyalists

1. What is the Orange Order and its significance?

The Orange Order was founded in 1795 in the County Armagh. It is dedicated to maintaining the link with Britain. No Catholic or anyone with Catholic relatives is allowed to join the order. It is fiercely anti-Catholic and constantly mobilizes the loyalists with its rhetoric, banners, sashes and parades. It has been associated with the Official Unionist Party and Protestant supremacy. Throughout the years, it has been used to destroy the development of class conscious political alliances between loyalists and nationalists. Since the 1970s, it has declined in strength in large part due to the split in the Official Unionist Party and the rise of the militant Ulster Defence Association (UDA). Its influence on the judicial system, however, remains strong.

2. Differentiate loyalist and unionist.

Unionists are those people in Ireland that desire to remain part of Britain.

Loyalists are unionists who are more militant and willing to use violence to maintain the Union with Britain.

The terms have been used interchangeably by many and differentiation is difficult.

3. Differentiate the three loyalist political parties.

Democratic Unionist Party (DUP) was founded in November, 1971 by Ian Paisley (p. 142, #8). It is a right-wing, anti-Catholic loyalist party. It is closely tied to the Free Presbyterian church, founded in 1951 by Ian Paisley. A number of its key leaders are ministers. It has become a formidable political force in British occupied Ireland.

Official Unionist Party (OUP) is the lineal descendant of the old Unionist Party that governed British occupied Ireland from 1921 until 1972. It has always been linked to the British Conservative Party and the landowner, industrialist and business classes. It suffered several splits in the 1970s with the present party emerging, and others, such as the Vanguard Party, disappearing.

Alliance Party was founded in 1970 as a moderate loyalist party. It does include some Catholics in its largely middle-class membership. It views itself as an alternative to so-called extreme unionists as well as nationalists. Its role in the province is marginal at best.

4. Identify the UDA, UFF, and UVF.

Ulster Defence Association (UDA) is a unionist paramilitary group founded in 1969 as a vigilante group and more formally organized in 1971. The UDA was a legal organization for 20 years and was the only paramilitary organization in the world with a listed phone number and address. It is a heavily armed, hardline unionist organization that controls the loyalist ghettos and has engaged in sectarian assassinations. It is responsible for the death of over 700 mostly uninvolved nationalists.

Ulster Freedom Fighters (UFF) is a non-organization that served as a front for UDA violence. It emerged in 1973 and engages in the murder of Catholics. It has allowed the UDA to announce its acts of violence as that of UFF and still remain legal. The UFF was banned by the authorities while the UDA parent organization remained legal until August 10, 1992. However given the known connections with security forces one must question how the ban will be enforced.

Ulster Volunteer Force (UVF) is a unionist group founded in 1966 by the notorious killer Gusty Spence. It has carried out a vicious campaign of sectarian assassinations of Catholic civilians. The UVF is extremely anti-socialist and has connections with the neo-nazi British National Front.

Red Hand Commandos is a loyalist paramilitary group founded in 1972 possibly by John McKeague, to carry out sectarian murders. It was declared illegal in 1973. The Red Hand has claimed responsibility for an increased number of recent sectarian murders. There is some evidence that the group is associated with the UVF.

5. **What was the Council of Ireland of the mid-1970s and what was its significance?**

The 26-county Irish Republic agreed to co-operate in combatting "terrorism" and acknowledged that unification could come only with the consent of the "Northern" Ireland majority. In exchange, the Council of Ireland was created to deal with the northern question. The Council was comprised of both six-county and 26-county representatives. Its participation would be limited to mundane issues such as tourism.

It was really designed to undermine the IRA, because power-sharing allowed the unionists to continue to control the government, and the Council of Ireland recognized partition. But loyalists opposed and overturned these "compromises" that would have secured their position and primacy of power. It would appear that allowing nationalists the right of democratic participation seemed to be too great a price.

6. **Why did power sharing and the Council of Ireland of the mid-1970s fail?**

The loyalist Ulster Workers Council (UWC) workers went on an all out strike on May 14, 1974 and thousands of loyalists did not appear for work May 15, 1974. In succeeding days it became more widespread and on May 27 led to the collapse of the power-sharing proposals put forward by the British government.

It was a very effective action because of widespread compliance and the fact that loyalists controlled important jobs due to discrimination. The UWC controlled indispensible services such as sanitation, communication and heating. It was in a position to ruin, not just disrupt, the six county economy. For example, if the Belfast pumps stopped, the city would begin to flood in its own wastes due to the city's low-lying position. The control of electricity was another crucial element.

At the same time paramilitaries took over loyalist areas and the British Army did not move against them.

7. *What was the position of the British Army during the strike?*

It refused to arrest the strike leaders and avoided confrontation with the strikers. It refused to dismantle barricades and issued passes for essential services such as gasoline and energy output to strikers.

8. *Who is Ian Paisley and what role does he play in the politics of the six counties?*

A minister in the fundamentalist Free Presbyterian church, who is noted for his vehemently anti-Catholic bigotry. He reportedly has significant political ties with right-wing fundamentalist groups in America. He was invited and attended Ronald Reagan's inaugural in 1980. He opposes the reunification of Ireland or the redress of Catholic grievances. He regularly flouts the law and encourages violence, yet he is spokesperson for a large number of loyalists in the six counties. He is also the head of the Democratic Unionist Party (DUP) (p.139, #3).

9. *What are the possible connections between the UDR and RUC and the loyalist paramilitaries such as the UDA and UVF?*

The UDA and UVF, especially the UDA, have some cross-membership with the RUC and UDR (now known as the Royal Irish Regiment, p. 131, #16.F).

The RUC and UDR have been known to pass on information about nationalists and their neighborhoods to the loyalist paramilitaries, such as the case of Belfast solicitor Pat Finucane who was gunned down in his home, and the bombing of Sinn Fein President Gerry Adams' house in 1993.

CHAPTER SEVENTEEN

Other political players

1. Who were the Peace People and why did their movement collapse?

It was a group founded in August, 1976, by Betty Williams, Mairead Corrigan and Ciaran McKeown. It organized peace marches and song fests, and opposed violence. The world media and the British government seized the opportunity to present the movement as an alternative to the legitimate struggle to end British rule in Ireland. In 1977, Williams and Corrigan won the Nobel Peace Prize.

But in Belfast, the nationalist community realized that their opposition to violence was one-sided. IRA violence was condemned and British Army violence ignored. The movement fell apart rapidly amidst accusations of collaboration with the British Army and personal misuse of the prize money intended for the movement's activities. Williams finally quit the movement in dispute over the H-Block issue which she did not support.

The movement today is at best a social work agency.

2. Identify the SDLP and its role in northeast Ireland.

The Social Democratic Labor Party (SDLP) was founded in August, 1970, by Paddy Devlin, Gerry Fitt and Austin Currie. It attracted people from the Labor and Nationalist Parties. Its politics have vacillated left and right, and from non-participation to cooperation with the Orange State.

Its constituency is largely Catholic middle class. John Hume is its current most effective spokesperson. Its sociopolitical policies are usually rather obscure, leaving room for opportunist exploitation of current issues. The involvement of John

Hume in recent peace efforts indicates a shift toward a more definitive stance on tough national issues.

3. What is the position of the Workers Party in northeast Ireland today?

The Workers Party (formerly Official Sinn Fein, "the Stickies") claims a Marxist orientation and was founded when the Sinn Fein Party split in late 1969-70. It rejects a military solution to partition and accepts the presence of the British Army. It is openly anti-republican and expelled members that supported the hunger strike of 1981. The group's para-military wing (Official IRA) has apparently withered and died. It is alienated from most of the nationalist community and lacks any real influence or power.

4. What has been the role of the Catholic church hierarchy in the last 25 years? Why?

The hierarchy in the north has been either collaborative or silent regarding violence against Irish republicans, while downplaying the British role in repression and violence against the nationalist community. Most recently the hierarchy has urged their flock to not vote for Sinn Fein candidates. The hierarchy appears unwilling to take on the British because of their privileged socioeconomic position and a wish to maintain their segregated school system.

5. What has been the role of the 26-counties government during the last 25 years? Why?

Successive 26-county governments have variably collaborated with the British in maintaining the border between north and south, and suppressing the growth of republicanism. The Fianna Fail Party has given lip service to republican sentiments when it has been in its best interest electorally. The Irish government spends a great deal of money maintaining the border, and in 1988 it went so far as to agree to extradite a Republican political prisoner, Robert Russell, to the north.

The 26-county government appears afraid of being drawn into the conflict directly. More importantly, strong economic ties with Britain discourage a too-militant approach on the north out of fear of economic reprisals. Further, many political career "statesmen" in the south fear the possible changed political nature of a united Ireland when a million and half northerners are added to the relatively small population of the 26 counties of 3.5 million. Recently though, the leadership of the republic of Ireland has taken a more aggressive approach to forcing a solution to British control of the six counties.

6. What is Section 31?

A section of the Irish Broadcasting Act that gives the 26-county government power to ban the broadcast of any material at will. It makes it possible to censor electronic media coverage of the struggle in the six counties. An amendment to Section 31 in October of 1976 banned interviews with members of the IRA as well as Sinn Fein. Thus it has prevented Sinn Fein, the main voice of Irish republicanism, from gaining access to the air waves. It has seriously limited the average citizen's knowledge of the magnitude and direction of the situation in northeast Ireland.

Early in 1994 Irish Arts & Culture Minister Michael Higgins proposed the repeal of Section 31 and it is currently suspended. However, other sections of the Irish Broadcasting Act may still be used to prohibit interviews the government deems promote violence, and Section 31 may be reactivated at any time.

7. What was the Anglo-Irish Agreement (Hillsborough Treaty)

An agreement signed in November of 1985 in Hillsborough, Ireland, by the London and Dublin governments. It granted the 26-county republic of Ireland a limited advisory in northeast Ireland, while keeping final authority in British hands. For example, the British denied a Dublin government request that three judges, instead of one, preside in the Diplock Courts. The agreement gained for England more cross-border cooperation in security, economics and cultural matters (especially security).

8. What has been the significance of the Anglo-Irish Agreement?

A. It attempted to make international critics think something was being done to solve the conflict.

B. It attempted to shore up the moderate politics of the SDLP by highlighting them as nationalist spokespersons.

C. It has resulted in a loyalist backlash that has resulted in the death of some nationalists and the burning out of others in some mixed areas.

D. It has also resulted in more cross border co-operation between the Irish and British governments.

9. What has been the role of the United States government?

A. Its diplomatic role has largely consisted of a hands-off policy, viewing it as a British internal disturbance.

B. The U.S. government has denied visas to nationalists attempting to enter the U.S. in order to present an alternative viewpoint.

C. The U.S. government has also cooperated with the British to harass and arrest Irish political prisoners who have sought asylum in the U.S. The case of Irish political prisoner Joe Doherty dragged on in the U.S. Courts for eight years before he was finally deported in 1992. During the Joe Doherty court battle, many U.S. courts ruled in his favor, citing U.S. laws that are meant to guarantee asylum to those seeking refuge from political persecution.

D. The U.S. government has harassed American citizens that have attempted to support Irish freedom fighters.

E. However, some individual American politicians such as Peter King, Thomas Manton, Hamilton Fish, Joseph Kennedy and others have been outspoken in their support for Irish freedom.

10. What are the MacBride Principles?

A set of principles formulated in the early 1980s by the late Sean MacBride aimed at encouraging fair employment in northeast Ireland. American companies doing business in northeast Ireland were urged to support the Principles, and intensive campaigns have been waged to pressure them to do so, mostly in the form of getting state and local governments to threaten to stop doing business with companies that don't abide by the Principles.

The Principles are as follows:

- Increase representation of individuals from underrepresented religious groups in the workforce including managerial, supervisory, administrative, clerical and technical jobs.

- Provide for adequate security for the protection of minority employees both at the workplace and while traveling to and from work.

- Ban provocative religious or political emblems from the workplace.

- All job openings should be publicly advertised and special recruitment efforts should be made to attract applicants from underrepresented religious groups.

- Layoff, recall, and termination procedures should not in practice favor particular religious groupings.

- Abolish job reservations, apprenticeship restriction, and differential employment criteria, which discriminate on the basis of religion or ethnic origin.

- Develop training programs that will prepare substantial numbers of current minority employees for skilled jobs, including the expansion of existing programs and the creation of new programs to train, upgrade and improve the skills of minority employees.

- Establish procedures to assess, identify and actively recruit minority employees with potential for further advancement.

- Provide the appointment of a senior management staff member to oversee the company's affirmative action efforts and the setting of timetables to carry out affirmative action principles.

To date at least 13 states and a number of cities have enacted MacBride legislation. In addition 25 U.S. and Canadian companies have agreed to implement the Principles. The British government has spent billions of dollars in the U.S. in an attempt to defeat the MacBride Principles, going to great lengths to argue they are unnecessary and unfair.

CHAPTER EIGHTEEN

The future course of the struggle

1. Why do some people refer to the two wars in northeast Ireland?

Because there are really two wars going on: One a liberation struggle between republican and British occupation forces. However, a second sectarian war is being carried on against the ordinary Catholic civilian population by loyalist paramilitary groups such as the UDA and the UVF. This second war has claimed the lives of over 600 uninvolved Catholics.

2. What are the three basic conditions that are the prerequisites to a final solution to the conflict?

A. A declaration of British withdrawal.

B. An all-Ireland election on the question of reunification.

C. Amnesty for all political prisoners.

3. Why do the British stay?

A. To protect what remains of British economic investments in northeast Ireland.

B. To protect NATO military interests since a united Ireland would be a non-aligned state.

C. To keep the whole island economically dependent on Britain, the six counties are held hostage.

D. Anti-Irish racism and bigotry characteristic of British history views the Irish as inferior and in need of guidance from Britain.

E. To preserve an imperial image of British prestige and power as well as to hold the last vestige of Britain's once global empire.

F. Loyalist votes help keep the conservative Tory Party in power.

4. Would there be a blood bath if the British withdrew?

A blood bath is already in progress and the occupation forces are responsible for a large number of casualties. As of 1993 over 3,000 lives have been claimed in the conflict. Loyalists have not died in the same numbers for their ideals as republicans have for the past 70 years. It is possible that without the support of Britain, loyalists might be forced to live with their fellow Irish.

It is possible for the British to withdraw with a minimal amount of violence. As they withdraw they should disarm the RUC and RIR (former UDR) thus preventing these sectarian forces from using British weapons in a reactionary backlash.

5. What about the idea that the majority must rule?

From its very beginning the six-county statelet had an artificially created loyalist majority that was the result of a well conceived political gerrymander (p. 107, #14). No one, north or south, ever voted to have Ireland partitioned. Loyalists were and still are a minority on the whole island. Until 1920 there was no Northern Ireland — even Britain governed the island as a single political unit until the Government of Ireland Act of 1920. If majority rule is to be valid, the people of the whole island, all 32 counties must vote on Irish unity.

To guarantee a loyalist veto over the wishes of the majority of the Irish people is undemocratic.

However, a loyalist majority in the six counties is no excuse for the way the nationalist minority has been and still is treated as second class citizens. Institutionalized discrimination and systematic disprivilege are not majority perogatives when dealing with minorities.

6. Is there support in the 26-counties for a united Ireland?

Various polls show that 70-80% of the people favor a united Ireland. This is true despite the fact that republicanism has been ruthlessly suppressed by the Irish police and censored by the govern ment in many shapes and forms. Even with the repal of Section 31 of the Radio and Television Act (p. 144, #6) the news remains managed to marginalize the nationalist struggle. However, during the hunger strikes of 1981, two political prisoners of war, Kieran Doherty and Paddy Agnew, were elected to the Irish Dail (Parliament). Support for the armed struggle is especially strong in the border counties and some national polls indicate the 30% of the population supports the goals of the armed campaign of the IRA.

7. What is the significance of Articles 2 and 3 of the Irish Constitution?

These articles from the Irish Constitution of 1937 define the national territory of Ireland as consisting of the whole island and that the six counties are under British control only temporarily pending re-integration to the national territory. Thus, according to its own Constitution, the republic of Ireland does not recognize the legitimacy of the British presence in northeast Ireland.

8. Is there popular support for withdrawal among the British people?

The struggle in the six counties is not against ordinary British people who have been largely left uninformed by government manipulation of the media and negative stereo-typing of the Irish. Opinion polls taken throughout the 1970s, 80s, and 90s by independent organizations such as Gallup, consistently indicate the English people are indeed war-weary and want their boys to come home — a phenomenon similar to the Viet Nam anti-war movement in the U.S. Grassroots political groups such as the Troops Out Movement (TOM) and Time to Go have campaigned for withdrawal. A number of ex-soldiers have written or spoken out against the war in northeast Ireland. The war in the six counties is with the British government and ruling class as well as with their locally recruited occupation forces the RUC and RIR (the former UDR) not the British people.

9. What is the Downing Street Declaration of December 15, 1993?

A joint declaration issued by Prime Minister John Major of Britain and Irish Taoiseach Albert Reynolds was purported to be an effort to bring all parties into peace talks. But it did not offer anything really new and failed to remove the loyalist veto over Irish unity and address the prospect of British withdrawal.

10. What was the Hume-Adams initiative?

Between 1991—1993 John Hume, leader of the moderate nationalist party the SDLP, and Gerry Adams, the leader of Sinn Fein, established a working relationship on the issue of the British presence in the six counties. The two leaders agreed that all parties must be part of a solution and that Britain must set in motion initiatives leading to their eventual withdrawal from Ireland.

11. What is the significance of the IRA ceasefire of August 31, 1994?

The IRA took away Britain's excuses for not wanting to talk about a solution to the situation in the six counties. The additional ceasefire announcement made by loyalist paramilitary groups on October 20, 1994, now clearly puts the ball in Britain's court. It may now be possible to work toward a process of national reconciliation and national self determination and the creation of an Irish national democracy.

12. What are the current prospects for peace in Ireland?

As this book goes to press in early 1995, many unprecedented events signal openings for peace. A framework document has been agreed to by the Irish and British governments, which at its core recognizes the failure of partition and the necessity for an all-Ireland dimension if there is to be peace. Irish Prime Minister Albert Reynolds held meetings with Sinn Fein President Gerry Adams, as has his successor John Bruton. Senior British officials have met with Sinn Fein delegations, but have refused as yet to meet at the ministerial level.

Sinn Fein officials have met with policy makers from many countries to build world opinion for a just peace settlement. Gerry Adams was granted a 48-hour visa to the U.S. in early 1994. This visit ended a U.S. policy of censorship of Irish republican views by visa denial. Sinn Fein now operates a Washington D.C. office to lobby American political support.

Gaining loyalist cooperation will be critical in achieving peace, and it appears the British government is still willing to grant a loyalist veto over any settlement that changes the status quo.

13. What are the major misconceptions regarding the situation in northeast Ireland?

A. That it is a religious based struggle (p. 109, #21).

B. That the British are impartial peacekeepers (p. 113, #7).

C. That the struggle lacks popular support in Ireland (p. 120, #10).

D. That it is a simple question of majority rule in the six counties (p. 150, #5).

E. That the British government would like to withdraw (p. 149, #3)

F. That there is no popular support in the 26 counties (p. 150, #6).

G. That a state of war does not exist (p. 126, #7; p. 129, #14).

H. That a bloodbath would follow British withdrawal (p. 150, #4).

I. That the struggle is part of an organized international conspiracy (p. 121, #11).

14. Is there a solution?

Yes, total British withdrawal and a democratic vote on the future of the whole island by the people of all 32 counties. Withdrawal could be initiated by setting a definite and reasonable date for disengagement. It should also include the disarming and disbandment of indigenous forces previously armed by Britain. International support to facilitate legitimate self-determination and resolution of conflicts between communities would also be key.

For further reading and study on the contemporary struggle

Adams, G. 1986. *The Politics of Irish Freedom.* Brandon, Cork.
Gerry Adams, the President of Sinn Fein, briefly outlines the political philosophy and socio-historical context of republican politics in Ireland. It clarifies and defends the aims of the republican movement. A well written, readable book.

Adams, G. 1988. *A Pathway to Peace.* Mercier, Cork.
A brief critique by Sinn Fein President Gerry Adams of the Hillsborough Treaty, Dublin's role, unionism and the various forms of nationalism without respect to the situation in the six counties. It includes his suggestions for movement toward a peaceful resolution.

Adams, G. 1990. *Cage Eleven.* Brandon, Dingle, Kerry.
A personal account of life in the cages of Long Kesh in the early 1970s.

Arthur, P. 1974. *The People's Democracy 1968-73.* Blackstaff Press, Belfast.
An analysis of a radical organization evolving in the midst of sociopolitical turmoil.

Asmal, K. 1985. *Shoot to Kill?* Mercier, Cork.
This is the report of the International Lawyers' Inquiry into the lethal use of firearms by security forces in Northern Ireland. It is based on the systematic assessment of 30 cases of unarmed civilians with no paramilitary connections who died at the hands of security forces. It includes information on more than 150 cases and concludes with recommendations on justice and the role of law in Northern Ireland.

Belfrage, S. 1987. *Living with War: A Belfast Year*. Penguin, NY.
An attempt by a noted journalist to objectively dissect the world of Belfast loyalists and nationalists. However, she fails. The author obviously spent more time and effort providing an indepth view of loyalists, and as a result the nationalist or republican viewpoint is superficial and predictable.

Bell, G. 1973. *The Protestants of Ulster*. Pluto Press, London.
An inside look at the Protestant mentality in Ulster by a fellow Protestant. It helps the reader understand the relationship of Protestantism to loyalism, providing a factual indictment of Ulster Protestant bigotry.

Bell, G. 1982. *Troublesome Business: The Labor Party and the Irish Question*. Pluto Press, London.
The first history of the Labour Party's attitude toward the Irish question. Bell argues that in general the Labour Party has defended the division of Ireland and that its actions have not been honorable. He further feels that the Party must confront the Irish issue if it is to fulfill its socialist mission and that the hunger strikes have made an impact in this direction among some members of the Party.

Bell, G. 1984. *The British in Ireland: A Suitable Case for Withdrawal*. Pluto Press, London.
A member of the British Labor Party forcefully argues for the need to make British withdrawal from Ireland a political priority.

Bell, J.B. 1980. *The Secret Army*. Mass. Instit. Tech. Press, Cambridge, Mass., 2nd ed.
A scholarly compendium on the history of the IRA, a good factual reference, but his analysis of the modern IRA ideology, strategy and grassroots support is weak.

Bell, J.B. 1987. *The Gun in Politics*. Transaction Books, New Brunswick NJ.
An academic analysis of the use of physical force in Irish Republican history. It is a dispassionate

factual account based on years of research on the IRA. It is a useful source of reference material on the Irish freedom struggle.

Bell, J.B. 1990. *IRA Tactics and Targets*. Poolbeg Swords, Ireland.
An attempt by a long-time scholar of the IRA to analyze the tactical aspects of the IRA's war against Britain. While interesting and somewhat stimulating it suffers from selective case bias and sometimes superficial subjective inter- pretations.

Bell, J.B. 1993. *The Troubles: A Generation of Violence 1967-1992*. St. Martins Press, New York.
A lengthy chronicle of the struggle in the six counties by a well-known author and self-proclaimed expert on the IRA. Bell see no solutions, blames the romanticism and violence of the Irish people and largely relieves Britian of much responsibility for the situation in northeast Ireland.

Beresford, D. 1987. *Ten Dead Men*. Grafton Books, London.
A detailed look at the 1981 Hunger Strike drawing extensively on secret IRA papers and letters smuggled out of the prison during the strike. A very human story told by a knowledgeable journalist.

Bew, P., P. Gibbon, and H. Patterson. 1979. *The State in Northern Ireland 1921-72 Political Forces and Social Classes*. Manchester University Press, Manchester.
A group of revisionist Marxist scholars attempts a Marxist analysis of the organizational basis of Unionism and the six county statelet. They stress a Protestant cross-class alliance, while admitting occasional interclass differences. It is a sophisticated but uncritical approach to Protestant working class sectarianism.

Bew, P. and H. Patterson. 1985. *The British State and the Ulster Crisis*. Verso, London.
A short Marxist history of the conflict in the six counties that is strongly anti-republican and especially hostile to Sinn Fein. It concludes just before the Hillsborough Treaty.

Boland, K. 1988. *Under Contract With The Enemy*. Mercier, Cork.
A brief booklet by Kevin Boland, a former Fianna Fail minister, that provides an in-depth analysis of the degeneration of Fianna Fail republicanism. An interesting account of the de-republicanization of a political party as it moves toward what appears to be an almost neo-colonial position.

Boland, K. 1985. *Great Is My Shame*. Rathcoole, Dublin.
A brief account by a former "establishment" republican of how the leadership of Ireland's conceding to British intransigence betrays the Irish past and prolongs the strife and bitterness.

Boyd, A. 1984. *Have the Trade Unions Failed in the North?* Mercier, Cork.
A brief history of trade unions in the six counties from a nationalist perspective. It is very critical of the trade union movement.

Boyle, K., T., Hadden and P. Hillyard. 1975. *Law and the State, the Case of Northern Ireland*. Martin Robinson, London.
The authors feel that the law is in alliance with a sectarian state. They also feel that the state is unstable and dependent upon coercion, not conciliation. Further, they conclude that security response of the state has impeded the restoration of stability.

Boyle, K. 1980. *Ten Years in Northern Ireland; The Legal Control of Political Violence*. Cobden Trust, London.
An examination by two lawyers and a sociologist of the legal measures taken to control violence in northeast Ireland. It examines the nature of the Diplock Courts, but assumes they are fair in handling republicans and loyalists alike. They are more critical of the functioning of the police and feel they are biased against nationalists. The authors also feel that some middle class Catholics have improved their position under direct rule, but most Catholics are no better off and in some cases worse off than they were under loyalist Stormont.

Burke, M. 1987. *Britain's War Machine in Ireland.* OISIN Publications, NY.
A brief introduction to the role of the British security forces in northeast Ireland.

Burke, M. 1990. *Britain in Ireland: The Facts.* OISIN Publications, NY.
A brief, clearly written account of the British occupation of the six counties written by an articulate priest activist. It is packed with facts on every important issue related to the struggle in the northeast of Ireland.

Burton, F. 1976. *The Politics of Legitimacy: Struggles in a Belfast Community.* Routledge and Kegan Paul, London.
A participant observation study of the sociopolitical development and struggles of the IRA in Ardoyne, a North Belfast nationalist community.

Campbell, B., L. McKeown and F. O'Hagan 1994. *Nor Meekly Serve My Time: the H-Block Struggle 1976-1981.* Beyond the Pale Publications, Belfast.
The story of the republican prison protest using the accounts of men who lived through and survived those years. A moving insight into why ten men gave their lives in pursuit of a political goal.

Campbell, F. 1992. *The Dissenting Voice: Protestant Democracy from Plantation to Partition.* Blackstaff, Belfast.
An history of the role of radical Protestants in the struggle against British imperialism.

Clarke, A.F.N. 1984. *Contact.* Schocken, NY.
An insider's view of life in the British Army in the six counties by a former soldier. It is significant because it illustrates the racism, bias and contempt that is rampant among the British troops in Ireland. It explains a lot of their actions.

Collins, M. 1985. *Ireland After Britain.* Pluto Press, London.
A collection of essays which discuss what will occur after Britain withdraws from Ireland. There

are 16 contributors from Gerry Adams to Mary Robinson to Tony Benn, representing a very diverse set of viewpoints.

Collins, T. 1983. *The Center Cannot Hold.* Bookworks Ireland, Dublin.
A popular work, accompanied by excellent photography that attempts to examine the past decade and half in northeast Ireland. The author points out the failures of the British government and proposes some possibilities for resolution. Even Andy Tyrie, the former head of the UDA, has praised the work.

Collins, T. 1986. *The Irish Hunger Strike.* White Island, Dublin.
A well-written account of the 1981 hunger strikers, with individual chapters on each of the ten men who died. It is based heavily on family interviews and presents a humanistic introduction to the subject, especially useful for those with little background in Irish history.

Coogan, T.P. 1980. *The IRA,* 2nd ed. Fontana Books, Douglas, Isle of Man.
A concise, well-written account of the IRA and the sociohistorical context in which it operates.

Coogan, T.P. 1980. *On the Blanket.* Ward River Press, Dublin.
A behind-the-scenes account of the blanket protest and an analysis of prison protest by the republican movement during the last 100 years.

Conroy, J. 1987. *Belfast Diary.* Beacon Books, Boston.
A personal account of the everyday lives and struggles of the people of Clonard by a sympathetic reporter, who spent a year in the district.

Coughlin, A. 1986. *Fooled Again? The Anglo-Irish Agreement and After.* Mercier , Cork.
An analysis of the Hillsborough Treaty by a well-known critic.

Coulter, C. 1992. *Web of Punishment: An Investigation*. ATTIC Press, Dublin.
A concise, clearly written work on the life of the Irish prisoners and their families. It consists of accounts by people who have been in prison or have relatives in prison. It highlights the web of punishment in which prisoners and their relatives are enmeshed. It argues for bringing Irish prisoners near home to serve their sentences in order to alleviate undue suffering to both prisoners and their families.

Cunningham, M. 1979. *Monaghan: County of Intrigue*. Abbey Printers, Cavan.
An account of the political and legal intrigue in the border area during the period 1968-1979. A useful view of Irish government collaboration and anti-republicanism.

Curtis, L. 1984. *Ireland: The Propaganda War. The British Media and the Battle for Hearts and Minds*. Pluto Press, London.
An account of how the British media have twisted and perverted British public opinion on northeast Ireland. It is a well researched work that is a powerful indictment of the so-called "free" press.

Curtis, L. 1984. *Nothing But the Same Old Story: The Roots of Anti-Irish Racism*. Information on Ireland, London.
A brief, well-written historical documentation of the role of anti-Irish racism in Anglo-Irish relations.

D'Arcy, M. 1981. *Tell them Everything*. Pluto Press, London.
The story of the Armagh women prisoners by a playwright who spent three months in the jail with them during the dirty protest. She questions the silence of feminists on the treatment of Republican women prisoners.

deBaroid, C. 1989. *Ballymurphy and the Irish War*. Aisling Publishers, Dublin.
A detailed historical account of the struggle in West Belfast from the pre-civil rights era to the present. A rich source of local history from the

ground up without the usual academic pretensions.

Devlin, B. 1969. *The Price of My Soul*. Knopf, NY.
An interesting biography of the early development of one of Ireland's most significant civil rights leaders. It is full of interesting insights and observations on the dynamics of the sectarian state.

Dunne, D. 1988. *Out of the Maze*. Gill and Macmillan, Dublin.
The story of the 1983 escape of 38 IRA members from Long Kesh, the biggest jail escape since World War II.

Ellis, Peter Beresford. 1972. *A History of the Irish Working Class*. George Braziller, NY.
The first major history of Ireland written by an Irish socialist since James Connolly's *Labor in Irish History* in 1910. A good general, easily read history of Ireland.

Fairweather, E., McDonough, R., and M. McFadyean. 1984. *Only the Rivers Run Free: Northern Ireland the Women's War*. Longwood Publishers, Wolfeboro, NH.
A well-written account of the situation that daily confronts women in the six counties.

Faligot, R. 1983. *Britain's Military Strategy in Ireland; The Kitson Experiment*. Brandon, Kerry, Eire.
This work is a detailed study of Britain's military operation in Ireland. The author, a noted Breton-French journalist, describes the application of Kitson's theory of low intensity operations in action. He further contends that the six counties have become a laboratory to experiment with new methods of controlling civilian populations.

Farrell, M. 1980. *Northern Ireland, the Orange State*. 2nd ed. Pluto Press, London.
A very good socialist history of the colonial situation in Ireland by a former member of the People's Democracy. Farrell also suggests a program of action.

Farrell, M. 1983. *Arming the Protestants: The Formation of the Ulster Special Constabulary and the Royal Ulster Constabulary 1920-27*. Brandon Books, Cork.
A former civil rights leader examines how the British government armed, financed and legalized Protestant paramilitary forces in the six counties during the 1920s. He also shows how British policy in the six counties turned the Catholic minority against the state. An important work for understanding the foundations of the present police state.

Farrell, M. 1985. *Sheltering the Fugitive: The Extradition of Irish Political Offenders*. Mercier, Cork.
An examination of the history and dynamics of extradition from Ireland and the United States to Britain from the 1850s to the 1980s.

Farrell, M. (ed.) 1988. *Twenty Years On*. Brandon, Dingle, Kerry.
Nine people who were involved in the civil rights movement look back over their participation in the struggle in the six counties over the last 20 years. Each individual from Bernadette Devlin McAliskey to Gerry Adams has an incisive chapter in this work.

Feehan, J.M. 1983. *Bobby Sands and the Tragedy of Northern Ireland*. Mercier Press, Cork.
An account of the life of Bobby Sands, in the sociohistorical context of the fascist statelet of "Northern" Ireland. An excellent introduction to Bobby Sands and his role as well as the overall concept of the revolutionary struggle in Ireland.

Fields, R. 1976. *Society Under Siege*. Temple University Press, Philadelphia.
A book originally suppressed in Britain, then printed in the USA. It is a telling analysis of the role of the British establishment in the application of systematic psychological genocide in the north of Ireland.

Fisk, R. 1975. *The Point of No Return: the Strike that Broke the British in Ulster*. Andre Deutsch, London.

The most comprehensive description of the loyalist strike of 1974 that helped to destroy power sharing proposals. It illustrates the no surrender mentality of loyalists and the refusal of the British Army to impose order by confronting the loyalists.

Flackes, W.D. and S. Elliott. 1988. *Northern Ireland: A Political Directory 1968-88*. Blackstaff, Belfast.
A basic reference source on the issues, individuals and groups involved in the struggle in the six counties. It is set up in a dictionary format making it useful for quick reference. The third edition.

Foot, P. 1988. *Who Framed Colin Wallace?* Macmillan, London.
A chilling expose by a British journalist that documents further aspects of the dirty undercover operations of the British in northeast Ireland.

Gallagher, F. 1957. *The Indivisible Island*. Gollancz, London.
An older work that describes the origins, development and reality of partition. An excellent source on the role of gerrymandering.

Gifford, T. 1984. *Supergrasses:The Use of Accomplice Evidence In Northern Ireland*. Cobden Trust, London.
A excellent review of the supergrass strategy with recommendations for reform.

Gillespie, A. and E. Gillespie. 1987. *Sisters in Cells*. FNT, Westport, Mayo, Ireland.
The story of two Irish republican womens' experiences in an English jail between 1974 and 1983, Aine and Eibhlin Gillespie of Donegal. Translated from the original Irish.

Greaves, C.D. 1974. *The Irish Crisis*. International Publishers, NY.
A socialist analysis from partition through the civil rights movement to the intervention by the British army. The result is a class-conscious history in socioeconomic context.

Holland, J.D. 1981. *Too Long a Sacrifice*. Dodd and Mead, NY.
An analytical look at the past decade by a former Belfastman now living in the United States. Especially good on the loyalist paramilitiaries but weak on the IRA today.

Holland, J.D. 1987. *The Irish-American Connection*. Viking Books NY.
A somewhat sensational attempt to examine Irish American involvement today. However it lacks depth and breadth of the movement in the United States.

Holroyd, F. 1989. *War Without Honor*.
A former British military intelligence officer describes British "dirty tricks" operations in both the six counties and the 26-county Irish republic. It provides a lot of insight on British intelligence operations in Ireland.

Jackson, T.A. 1970. *Ireland Her Own*. International Publishers, NY.
A detailed outline of Irish history by English socialist and partisan of Irish freedom beginning with ancient Ireland up to partition. An epilogue by C. Desmond Greaves covers the period from partition to the Northern Ireland civil rights movement is included in the new paperback edition. An excellent anecdote to the rampant revisionism of today.

Jennings, A. (ed.) 1988. *Justice Under Fire: The Abuse of Civil Liberties in Northern Ireland*. Pluto, London.
A series of analyses by various experts on emergency laws, Diplock Courts, the supergrass system, shoot to kill, the PTA and plastic bullets. The political and social dimensions of systematic disregard of basic human rights are emphasized.

Kelly, K. 1982. *The Longest War: Northern Ireland and the IRA*. Brandon Book Co., Dingle, Derry.
A history and analysis of the struggle in British-occupied Ireland by an uninvolved journalist. While generally sympathetic toward the Provi-

sional IRA, the author does present criticisms of their activities when appropriate.

Kitson, F. 1971. *Low Intensity Operations.* Faber and Faber, London.
The theoretical basis of Britain's approach in occupied Ireland is presented here, by a British counterinsurgency expert.

Lee, A.M. 1983. *Terrorism in Northern Ireland.* General Hall, NY.
A noted American scholar presents a humanistic analysis of the struggle in Ireland. It is one of the only works of this nature that views the British Army's role in Ireland as that of terrorists. It is thoroughly researched and a well-documented source of reference material.

Lindsay, K. 1980. *Ambush at Tully West: The British Intelligence Services in Action.* Dunrod Press, Newtownabbey, Antrim.
A book written by a loyalist that describes the "dirty tricks" tactics of the British in Ireland. Such tactics include bombing innocent people, killing unionists or Provos and blaming the other side, as well as constant intimidation of ordinary people.

McAuley, C. 1990. *Women in a War Zone.* Republican Publications, Dublin.
A brief book that documents the last 20 years of resistance to Britain from a woman's perspective. Many interesting photos and quotations are included.

McCafferty, N. 1981. *The Armagh Women.* Co-Op Books, Dublin.
One of the few descriptive accounts of the plight of the republican women in the Armagh jail. The author is an Irish feminist rather than a republican.

McCafferty, N. 1988. *Peggy Deery: An Irish Family at War.* Attic Press, Dublin.
A well-written account of the impact of the war on the family of Peggy Deery, a Derry woman.

McCann, E. 1980. *War in an Irish Town*, 2nd edition. Pluto Press, London.
A personal memoir and political analysis of growing up in a Catholic ghetto in northeast Ireland by a leader of the civil rights movement. It is also a really good story of how to build a revolutionary party. This new edition includes an analysis of the provisional IRA. It is probably necessary to read the first edition (1974) in order to get the full story.

McCann, E. 1992. *Bloody Sunday in Derry: What Really Happened*. Pluto Press, London.
A new look at the Bloody Sunday massacre of 1972 by a Derry-born journalist and activist. McCann calls for the reopening of the case and repudiation of the state's official whitewash, the Widgery Report.

McCardle, P. 1984. *The Secret War*. Mercier, Cork.
A brief book that documents the collaborative activities of the Gardai, RUC, British Army and SAS along the Irish border. It raises many sinister issues for consideration.

McEoin, G. 1974. *Northern Ireland: Captive of History*. Holt, Rhinehart, & Winston, New York.
A well written general survey of Irish history in a northern context from 1171 to Bloody Sunday. The author is a journalist who hoped for a federal state like Switzerland as an answer to the situation in northeast Ireland.

McGuffin, J. 1974. *The Guinea Pigs*. Penguin, London.
A study of torture during interrogation by the British in northeast Ireland.

McGuffin, J. 1973. *Internment*. Anvil. Tralee, Kerry.
The story of the use of internment as a political weapon from 1916 to 1973 both north and south of the Irish border.

McVeigh, J. 1989. *A Wounded Church: Religion, Politics and Justice in Ireland*. Mercier Press, Cork.
Father Joseph McVeigh attacks the response of the Catholic church in the situation in the north. He is

particularly critical of the church hierarchy who have become tools of the British because they are too concerned with their own power and special status.

Metress, S.P. 1983. *The Hunger Strike and the Final Struggle.* Connolly Books, Detroit.
A brief introduction to the history, ideology and impact of the hunger strike as a weapon in the Irish struggle for liberation.

Miller, D.W. 1978. *Queens Rebels: Ulster Loyalism in Perspective.* Gill and Macmillan, Dublin.
One of the few attempts to examine the history and myth structure of Irish loyalists in order to understand the passionate loyalty of many Northern Irish Protestants to the British crown.

Milligan, M., ed. 1981. *Ireland Unfree: Essays on the History of the Irish Freedom Struggle 1169-1981.* Pathfinder Press, Sydney, Australia.
A series of essays that trace the long struggle for Irish freedom from the Norman invasion to the hunger strikes of 1981.

Moloney, E. and A. Pollock. 1987. *Ian Paisley.* Poolbeg, Dublin.
A biography of the leader of militant loyalism by two Irish journalists. It provides a useful exposé of militant loyalist thinking.

Morgan, A. and B. Purdie eds. 1980. *Ireland: Divided Nation, Divided Class.* INK Links, London.
A collection of articles by Marxist scholars that includes pieces by both revisionist Marxists such as Bew, Gibbon and Patterson and traditionalists such as Farrell, Lysaght, Hoffman. Most of the essays argue that a fusion of Marxism and republicanism is not the future of revolutionary politics in Ireland. But essays by Farrell on the RUC, Ward on the role of women and Reid on the concept of labor aristocracy make the collection useful.

Mullin, C. 1987. *Error of Judgement.* Poolbeg Press, Dublin.
An account of the arrest, framing and miscarriage

of justice for six Irishmen related to the Birmingham Pub bombings of 1974.

Munck, R. 1986. *Ireland Nation, State and Class Struggle*. Westview Press, Boulder, CO.
A brief, well organized history of the northern struggle in the context of the Irish as well as local history by a socialist scholar sympathetic to the republican position.

Munck, R. 1993. *The Irish Economy: Results and Prospects*. Pluto Press, London.
A clear, concise analysis of the economy of Ireland as a whole from a "dependency development" perspective. A good source for those interested in the problems facing a united Ireland when it is a reality.

Murphy, D. 1991. *The Stalker Affair and the Press*. Unwin Hyman, London.
A detailed account of the development of a procedural scandal and the removal and discrediting of a respected police investigator John Stalker. It is a powerful indictment of British politics and society.

Murray, R. 1990. *The SAS in Ireland*. Mercier Press, Cork.
A detailed, heavily documented study of the activities of the SAS in the six counties by a respected activist priest, Father Raymond Murray. It details intelligence gathering, surveillance, connections with British intelligence as well as sectarian murders and their organized shoot to kill policy. A powerful indictment of their operations in an undeclared war.

O'Brien, J. 1989. *British Brutality in Ireland*. Mercier Press, Cork.
A history of British military and political policies in Ireland from the Normans to the 1988 Gibralter killings. A chilling story of brutality and misdeeds.

O'Dowd, L., B. Rolston and M. Thomlinson, eds. 1980. *Northern Ireland Between Civil Rights and Civil*

War. CSE Books, London.
A collection of readings that examine the British policy in the six counties since the fall of Stormont. It is a valuable update on this aspect of the conflict. Its major weakness lies in the failure to consider the impact and role of the republican movement on the dynamics of the six county statelet.

O'Farrell, P. 1975. *England and Ireland Since 1800.* Oxford University, London.
A concise history of English/Irish interaction since 1800, written by a distinguished scholar from Australia. It is an excellent source for depicting the English perceptions and priorities with respect to Ireland.

O'Malley, P. 1990. *Biting at the Grave.* Beacon Press, Boston.
An arrogant, unsympathetic revisionist account of the hunger strikes by an academic opportunist.

O'Sullivan, M. 1972. *Patriot Graves.* Follett, Chicago.
A marvelous photo essay of the early years of the struggle in the six counties by a photojournalist. He took great risks to produce this work. Both the photos and textual material are excellent.

Patterson, H. 1980. *Class, Conflict and Sectarianism: the Protestant Working Class and the Belfast Labour Movement 1868-1920.* Blackstaff, Belfast.
A poorly written work by a Marxist revisionist that views the divisions in Ireland as the result of different economic interests north and south developed in the 19th century. He denies the idea that working class people in six counties are dupes of the bourgoisie. Patterson also sees the Orange Order as not uniformly reactionary but as an expression of class conflict.

Probert, B. 1978. *Beyond Orange and Green: The Political Economy of the Northern Ireland Crisis.* ZED Press, London.
An attempt by a revisionist Marxist scholar to analyze the political economy beyond the split in the working class between the Orange "majority" and Green "minority." However Probert focuses

on the internal politics of the Protestant working class, with minimal analysis of Catholic working class disadvantage. She also isolates her analysis from an overall Irish political context.

Republican Prisoners of War 1987. *Questions of History Part I.* Sinn Fein, Dublin.
A history of the Irish Republican Movement written by their prisoners of war. It is an attempt to understand the present by questioning the past. It covers the period from Grattan's Parliament in the late 1700's to 1934 and the Republican Congress. An excellent example of grassroots social history.

Renwick, A. 1989. *Last Night Another Soldier.* Information on Ireland, London.
A short historical novel on the interaction between the British soldiers and the people of the north by an ex-British soldier.

Rolston, B.(ed) 1991. *The Media and Northern Ireland: Covering the Troubles.* Macmillan, London.
A collection of essays on how the media has covered the conflict in the six counties. The individual contributions cover topics such as Section 31, a profile of the three Belfast daily papers, the Gibralter killings, the failure of the American press and photographic images.

Rolston, B. 1991. *Politics and Painting: Murals and Conflict in Northern Ireland.* Associated Universities Press, Cranbury NJ.
An academic analysis of the history, and significance of mural painting in the six counties.

Rolston, W. ed. 1983. *A Social Science Bibliography of Northern Ireland 1945-1983.* Queens University, Belfast.
A comprehensive listing of a wide variety of references on the conflict up to 1983. An excellent source to begin a literature search on many aspects of the struggle.

Rowthorn, B. and N. Wayne. 1988. *Northern Ireland, the Political Economy of Conflict.* Westview Press, Boulder CO.

A detailed academic analysis of the political economy of the six counties from partition to the present. The authors argue for British withdrawal and reunification of Ireland. It is a clearly written, well documented and exceptionally reasoned account of the past, present and future of the six counties.

Sands, B. 1983. *One Day in My Life*. Mercier Press, Cork.
An account of one day in the prison life of Bobby Sands based on material smuggled out of the prison.

Sands, B. 1982. *Skylark Sing Your Lonely Song: An anthology of the Writings of Bobby Sands*. Mercier, Cork.
A collection of Bobby Sands' essays and poems with an interesting introduction by Ulick O'Connor.

Sands, B. 1981. *The Writings of Bobby Sands*. Irish Northern Aid, NY.
A collection of the prison essays of Bobby Sands that disclose the philosophy and convictions of a revolutionary.

Sands, B. 1981. *The Diary of Bobby Sands*. Sinn Fein, Dublin.
The first 17 days of Bobby Sands' hunger strike written in diary form.

Schlesinger, P., G. Murdock and P. Elliot. 1983. *Televising Terrorism: Political Violence in Popular Culture*. Commedia Publ. Group, London.
A detailed handbook of how the media and government manipulate the news. An especially good exposé of British methods of censorship.

Sluka, J. 1989. *Hearts and Minds, Water and Fish: Support for the IRA and INLA in a Northern Irish Ghetto*. JAI Press, Greenwich CT.
A scholarly study based on anthropological fieldwork in Belfast on the dynamics of support for republican paramilitiaries in Divis Flats.

Smith, C. 1989. *Ian Paisley: Voice of Protestant Ulster*. Scottish Academic Press, Edinburgh.
A highly complementary biography of Ian Paisley written by a longtime friend and associate. It allows one to view Paisley from the perspective of Free Presbyterianism and the Democratic Unionist Party.

Stalker, J. 1988. *The Stalker Affair*. Viking, NY.
The best selling story of Thatcher's cover-up of the Stalker investigation into charges of shoot to kill policies against the RUC.

Stewart, AT.Q 1977. *The Narrow Ground: Aspects of Ulster, 1609-1969*. Faber & Faber, London.
A readable account that articulates a Unionist view of Catholic-Protestant interaction in the six counties.

Taylor, P. 1980. *Beating the Terrorists: Interrogations in Omagh, Gough and Castlereagh*. Penguin, London.
A British journalist details police (RUC) mistreatment of suspects when held for questioning. It is carefully researched and examines the origins, progress and methods of the epidemic of violence during 1977-79 related to police interrogation. However, the author makes the incorrect assumption that it has ceased.

VanVoris, W.H. 1975. *Violence in Ulster: An Oral Documentary*. University of Massachusetts, Amherst.
A chronological documentary based on the memories of those who lived through the troubles from 1943 to 1972. The Irish speak for themselves so it depicts a raw taste of northeast Ireland. The interviews are a rich source of the meaning and ethos that are an integral part of the conflict.

Wallace, M. 1982. *British Government in Northern Ireland: From Revolution to Direct Rule*. David and Charles, Newton Abbot.
An Ulster-born journalist concentrates on British government policies from 1968 to the end of the hunger strike of 1981. It describes all the various

British government papers, reports and acts of Parliament. It contains little on local developments, but is a useful source for the British documents.

Walsh, D. 1983. *The Use and Abuse of Emergency Legislation in Northern Ireland*. Cobden Trust, London.
A survey of the administration of justice in northeast Ireland that describes in depth the continuing abuses of civil liberties.

White, B.W. 1993. *Provisional Irish Republicans: An Oral and Interpretative History*. Greenwood Press, Westport, Connecticut.
The best analysis of the Provisional IRA by a young academic who did fieldwork in the six counties.

Wilson, D. 1984. *Against Violence in Ireland*. Andersonstown News, Belfast.
A collection of talks given to American groups working for democracy in Ireland by Desmond Wilson, a priest from West Belfast who serves the nationalist/working class community. It also contains Wilson's submission to the New Ireland Forum.

Wilson, D. 1985. *An End to Silence*. Royal Carbery Books, Cork.
A brief account of the how the church and the government are the real causes of suffering and violence in northeast Ireland, not the paramilitaries on either side.

Index

A

Absentee landlords 36
Act of Settlement 30
Act of Union 44, 45, 52, 53
active service units 119
Adams, Gerry 142, 152
Agnew, Paddy 151
agrarian secret societies 34, 36
Allen, William 75
Alliance Party 140
American Civil War 74
American Commission for Relief in Ireland 92
American Commission on Conditions in Ireland 92
American Irish Political Education Committee 122
Amnesty International 128, 129, 137
An Cumann Cabhrach 121
ANC 121
Ancient Order of Hibernians (AOH) 87
Anglo-Irish Agreement 145, 146
Anglo-Irish War (1919-21) 86, 91, 92, 103, 104
Article 2, Irish constitution 151
Article 3, Irish constitution 151

B

B-Specials 108, 112, 113, 130
Ballot Act of 1872 78
Basques 121
Battle of Diamond 37
Battle of Kinsale 19, 21
Battle of the Boyne 32
Bell Beaker people 2
Bell, J. Bowyer 117
Bennett Report 129

Biggar, Joseph 78
Bill of Indictment 132
Black and Tans 92, 93, 102, 104
Black Death 16
Blake, John Dillon 72
blanket men 126
blanket protest 126
Blanqui, Auguste 76
blood bath theory 150
Bloody Sunday, January, 1972 113
Boer War 86
Boers 84
Border War, 1950s 115
Boundary Commission of 1925 97
Brehon laws 14
Brehons 3
Bretons 121
Brian Boru 8
British Army in Northern Ireland 113, 124
British-occupied Ireland 123
Bronze Age 1
Brookeborough, Lord 107
Bruce, Edward 13, 16
Bull of Laudabiliter 10
Burntollet Bridge, civil rights march attacked at 112
Butt, Isaac 78

C

Campaign for Social Justice 111
Capt. Moonlight 34
Carson, Edward 87
Catholic Association 50, 51
Catholic Church 144
    and the Fenian movement 72
    and the Gaelic League 85
Catholic Confederation (1642) 25
Catholic Emancipation 49, 50
Catholic Relief Act of 1829 51
Catholic Relief Bill of 1793 38, 51
Catholicism, Irish celtic 6
Celts 2-4
Charles I 24
Charles II 29
Christianity in Ireland 6

Fenian insurrection, 1867 74
Fenian movement 71, 76
   and the U.S. Civil War 74
feudalism 16
Fianna Fail 98, 144
Finucane, Pat 142
Fish, Hamilton 146
Fitt, Gerry 143
Fitzgerald, Edward 74
Fitzgerald, Thomas. *See Silken Thomas*
Flags and Emblems Act of 1954 138
Flannery, Michael 121
Flight of the Earls 20, 21, 23
Flight of the Wild Geese 32
Flood, Henry, 38
Francis, John McQuire 72
Free Irish Parliament Act of 1783 37
Free Presbyterian church 139, 142
Free State government 98
French Revolution 38, 39
Friends of Irish Freedom 94

G

Gaelic Athletic Association (GAA) 85, 89
gaelic culture in Ireland 14
Gaelic League 85, 89
Gaels 5
Garibaldi 73
General Humbert 42
gerrymandering 106, 111, 113, 150
Gladstone, British Prime Minister 77, 81, 82
Glover Report 117, 120
"God Save Ireland" 75
Goulding, Cathal 114, 115
Government of Ireland Act of 1920 104, 150
Grand Orange Order of Ulster *See Orange Order*
Grattan, Henry 38, 44, 49, 88
Green Cross 121
Griffith, Arthur 88, 91

H

Hay, John 87
Healy, Tim 84
"Hell or Connaught" 27
Henry II 10, 11
Henry VII 16
Henry VIII 16, 17
Hibernian Rifles 89
Higgins, Michael 145
Hillsborough Treaty. *See* Anglo-Irish Agreement
Hobson, Bullmer 88
Holland, John 78
Home Government Association 78
Home Rule 78, 79, 84, 87, 103
house searches 136
Hume, John 143, 152
Hume-Adams initiative 152
hunger strikes of 1980-81 127
hunger strikes of 1981 127, 128
Hyde, Douglas 85

I

internment 117
IRA *See Irish Republican Army (IRA)*
Ireland Act of 1949 99
Ireland, the Propaganda War 133
Ireton, General 27
Irish American Unity Conference (IAUC) 122
Irish Americans 122
Irish Citizen Army 89, 102, 103
Irish Civil War (1922-23) 94, 96, 97, 105
Irish Confederation 54, 55
Irish federalism 78
Irish Free State 95, 97, 99, 105
Irish Independence Party 119
Irish National Liberation Army (INLA) 118, 128
Irish Northern Aid Committee 121, 122
Irish Party *See* Irish Parliamentary Party
Irish Parliamentary Party 55, 78, 79, 82, 84

N

Nation, The 54
National Association 72
National Front 140
Nationalist Party 114, 119
nationalists 110, 121
Navigation Act 1663 29
Neave, Airey 118
New Departure policy *79*
Nine Years War 20
Noraid. *See* Irish Northern Aid
    Committee
Normans 10, 11, 12, 13, 15
northeast Ireland 122
Northern Ireland
    94, 104, 106, 107, 108, 109, 111,
    112, 122
Northern Ireland Civil Rights
    Association (NICRA) 111
Northern Ireland Emergency
    Provisions Act of 1973 124
Northern Star, The 39
Nugent, Kieran 126

O

Oak boys 36
Oath of Allegiance 95, 99, 105
O'Brien, Michael 75
O'Brien, William 54, 55, 84
O'Connell, Daniel
    48, 49, 50, 52, 53, 54
O'Dochartaigh, Fionbarra 108
O'Donnell, Hugh 19
O'Donnell, Rory 20
Offenses Against the State Act 130
Official Unionist Party (OUP) 139,
    140
O'Fiaich, Cardinal 127
Oglaigh na h Eireann. *See* Irish
    Republican Army (IRA)
O'Growney, Eugene 85
O'Hanlon, Feargal 115
O'Leary, John 72
O'Mahoney, John 72, 74
"one man, one vote" 111

O'Neil, Phelim 24
O'Neill, Hugh *19*
O'Neill, Owen Roe 25, 26
O'Neill, Shane 19
O'Neill, Terrence 108
Operation Motorman 135
opinion polls 151
Orange Order 37, 108, 139
O'Reilly, Myles 72
O'Shea, Captain 82
O'Shea, Kitty 82

P

Paisley, Ian 139, 142
Pale, the 12, 13, 16, 17
Paris revolt of 1848 55
Parliamentary election of 1918
    91, 102
Parnell, Charles 79, 80, 81, 82, 84
Partition 102
Peace People 143
Pearse, Padraic 43, 46, 85, 89, 90
Peel, Robert 53, 64
Peep-O-Day Boys 34, 37
Penal Codes 33, 34, 51
Peoples Democracy (PD) 118
Peters Pence 10
Phoenix Society 71
Pitt, William 43, 44
plantation of Ulster 23
plastic bullets 134
PLO 121
Plunkett, Bishop Oliver 29
Plunkett, Horace 86
pogroms of 1920-21 107
pogroms of 1969–1971 112
Polisario 121
Poor Commission 67
Poor Law Amendment of 1847 66
Pope Alexander III 10
potato in Ireland 36, 58, 59
Powderly, T.V. 77
Power, John *78*
Poynings Law 16, 31, 37
pre-Celtic Ireland 1
Prevention of Terrorism Act 126,